THE CONSOLATIONS OF MORTALITY

ANDREW STARK

The Consolations
of Mortality

Making Sense of Death

Yale UNIVERSITY PRESS

NEW HAVEN AND LONDON

Yale University Press books may be purchased in quantity for educational, business, or promotional use. For information, please e-mail sales.press@yale.edu (U.S. office) or sales@yaleup.co.uk (U.K. office).

Set in Janson Oldstyle and Futura Bold types by Newgen North America.
Printed in the United States of America.

Library of Congress Control Number: 2016934661
ISBN 978-0-300-21925-8 (cloth : alk. paper)

A catalogue record for this book is available from the British Library.

This paper meets the requirements of ANSI/NISO Z39.48-1992 (Permanence of Paper).

10 9 8 7 6 5 4 3 2 1

For Deborah

CONTENTS

ACKNOWLEDGMENTS

I am grateful to Hamish Clark, Isaac Clark, Fardowsa Hashi, Vladimir Helwig, Gavin Lee, and Yuki Nishimura for their superb research assistance, and to Jennifer Banks, Laura Davulis, Heather Gold, and Jeffrey Schier of Yale University Press for their support and wise editorial advice. I also thank Don Herzog, Mark Lilla, Patrick Luciani, William Ian Miller, Benjamin Mitchell-Yellin, Deborah Moores, Cliff Orwin, Donna Orwin, Rachel Stark, and Zoe Stark for their valuable and insightful comments on earlier versions. I have tried to implement their sage suggestions. I also, with deep appreciation, remind them of Otis Redding's great truth: "I can't do what ten people tell me to do/So I guess I'll remain the same."

THE CONSOLATIONS OF MORTALITY

INTRODUCTION

For those of us who are not believers—for those of us who suspect that death really is the final curtain—the wisdom of the ages has generated four great consolations for mortality: four distinct ways of persuading us to accept, maybe even appreciate, the fact that we will die. None of the four relies on religious conviction. None invokes the possibility of an afterlife. Each comes in multiple exotic guises. All have been around, in some form or another, for a long time. Centuries. Millennia, even, with sprawling roots in the ancient west, the timeless east, and the modern world.

Do they work? Can any one of the four really deliver on its promise to make us feel content, even at peace, with our inevitable demise? It's an important question. In fact, it's an urgent one.

In 1783 a French noblewoman sat in her carriage at the Tuileries, observing for the first time a hot-air balloon rise into the sky: a demonstration, she thought, of the kind of breakthroughs that science was on the verge of making. But the lady wasn't happy. "Oh yes, now it's certain!" she cried: "One day they'll learn to keep people alive forever, but I shall already be dead!"[1]

Given the pace and promise of biomedical innovation, a moment may well arrive when great numbers of our species start to feel like the lady: sensing that open-ended human longevity looms as an increasingly imminent possibility, yet fearing that they themselves might just miss out on it. For all who hold this worldview, the question of how to come to terms with their deaths will assume a desperate psychological urgency. And what if such a moment doesn't arrive any time soon? What if the riddle of mortality continues to elude cutting-edge science? Then the matter of reckoning with our finality will simply maintain the paramount importance it's always had.

Either way, we will want consolation. But are the four approaches that the ages bequeath to us up to the task? Does one perhaps work better than the others? Or is it just possible that something else entirely—maybe something that emerges only when the four are considered together—makes a compelling case that dying is better for us than any conceivable alternative?

By "us," I mean we bundles of ego and anxiety who love life, believe that death spells permanent obliteration, and live in the early twenty-first century. Strong egos that we are, we anguish as our precious selves move, inescapably and second by second, forward in time toward their impending ends. Lovers of life that we are, we agonize as its moments slip one by one, through our fingers, back into the irrecoverable past. How could *we* ever come to terms with such a reality?

The first of the four consolations tells us forthrightly that if we look at our situation in the right light, we will see that *death itself is actually a benign or even a good thing*. Philosophers from Epicurus to Heidegger to contemporary Buddhists have found different glimmers of this silver lining in our mortal condition. Epicurus, for example, counseled that the relationship between a person and his death is roughly akin—if I can use an analogy that was unavailable to Epicurus himself—to the relationship between Superman and Clark Kent. Whenever one is present, the other is nowhere to be seen. As long as a person is alive, his death has not yet happened. And then once his death occurs, he is no longer around to suffer it. Since our self can never encounter its own demise, Epicurus concluded, death should cause us absolutely no concern. It's entirely and utterly benign. The trick simply lies, Epicurus felt, in allowing the logical force of this observation to overcome the psychological terror that death inspires.

Existentialists and Buddhists assign death a benign countenance for a different kind of reason. As they see it, the relationship between death and the self is more like the Beatles' songwriting partnership between Lennon and McCartney. Only if Lennon is present in the credits will you find McCartney there too. And if there is no

McCartney in the byline, then there is no Lennon either. Likewise, only because death is present in the world, existentialists say, are selves present too. Because there is no such thing as the self to begin with, Buddhists counter, there is no such thing as death either.

Why, for existentialists, are death and the self joined at the hip? Because only if we remain constantly aware that our time is limited will we feel any urgency to get started in the world, make hard choices about what's important to us, and carve out the narrative arc of our own singular self. If by contrast no final deadline loomed, then we would endlessly dally and dawdle, failing to make anything of ourselves—or even make our selves in the first place. If we think about it deeply enough, we will see that mortality is thus a good thing. It's necessary to our very existence. Only because death exists does our self exist too.

Buddhism, by contrast, tells us that the self is an illusion. And so death, which is supposedly the destruction of the self, must be naught as well. There's nothing that it terminates. If there is no self, then all we are is a chain of moment-by-moment memories, experiences, hopes, dreams, thoughts, aspirations, and feelings over time. And all of them can survive our death, living on into the future in anyone who continues to share them. So we lose nothing to death. The trick lies simply in learning how to accept this truth.

Despite their stark differences, what philosophers espousing this first consolatory stream all argue—whether they are Epicurean, existentialist, or Buddhist—is that death is benignly irrelevant, maybe even positively good, for the person who dies. And there's no reference to an afterlife to be found in the lot of them.

The second consolatory stream flows in a different direction. According to its various advocates, all of the good things that we associate with death's alternative—namely, immortality—are actually fully available to us within the confines of our mortal life. *Within mortal life as it is, we can acquire all the intimations of immortality we could ever desire.* Since a well-lived mortal life offers everything that immortality could, death deprives us of nothing.

Think of the Microsoft techno-guru Gordon Bell. He promises that one day soon, thanks to 24/7 real-time video and audio recording, we will be able to upload everything that ever happens to us—in effect, the entire contents of our memories—online, to be preserved forever. E. M. Forster was crushed by the thought that once he expired, so too would all the precious reminiscences he cherished of his beloved mother. But, Bell claims, we can now obtain at least that particular benefit of immortality—the eternal preservation of our own irreplaceable trove of knowledge about the past—even if we die. We can all, Bell says, "off-load our memory" and thus gain "a kind of immortality."[2]

What other goods do we associate with continuing to live on indefinitely? Well, not only do we want to preserve what we and only we know about the past—our treasured memories—but we also want to know all about the future: we want to know every secret of the universe and God and consciousness that our species might one day discover. We also want to continue not just to know but to shape the future, to stamp our imprint on it, instead of being condemned, as we mortals sadly are, to having all traces of our existence eventually fade away as if we had never lived. And we will always need more time to shape not just the future but the past, to stamp our imprint on *it*, instead of being condemned, as we mortals distressingly are, to leaving mistakes unrepaired, regrets unamended, and defeats unvindicated.

But there are those who argue that if we look at matters in the right way, we will see that each of these good things, too, can be had within a mortal life every bit as much as we could get them (and maybe part of the issue is that we exaggerate how much we could get them) in an immortal life. Death could vanish, and we mortals would gain nothing—at least nothing of any value—that we don't already have. We should be consoled by this thought.

Immortality not only comes with good things, though. It's also wedded to some very bad ones. You might think that endless life is what you want. But beware of what you wish for. On the third broad stream of consolation, *immortality itself would actually be an awful fate,*

4

and so mortality is much to be preferred. Here again, thinkers have offered an array of possibilities.

Assume, for example, that as an immortal you retained an ongoing memory of everything that you experienced over the millennia. Then would you not come to feel, sooner or later as time marched on, as if you had seen everything that there is to see? And suppose, too, that you retained the same unvarying set of core desires and values as thousands upon tens of thousands of years passed. Then would you not come to feel, sooner or later, as if you had done all that you ever cared to do? And so wouldn't immortality ultimately spell interminable, excruciating boredom?

Suppose, though, that you dodged that fate. Suppose, as an immortal, that your oldest memories regularly vanished into the mists of time, so that the world always seemed to offer fresh experiences—experiences you wouldn't remember having had before. And suppose too that your desires and values repeatedly turned over, to be replaced by entirely new sets of ambitions and aspirations to pursue. Then, yes, you might well cheat boredom. But it would also be as if you were periodically dying to be reborn as someone totally different: someone with remembrances and goals utterly unrecognizable to your prior self, whose own memories and passions would in turn have been completely eradicated, consigned to oblivion. And then would immortality really be any different from mortality?

Still others say: maybe immortality would split the difference. Suppose that as an immortal you retained all of your memories from the earliest days onward, and that all your original desires and values, too, persisted indefinitely. You would certainly continue to be the same person. But suppose as well that novel challenges still continued to confront you, thanks to the disruptive mindsets of new generations or the ceaseless upheavals of a volatile biophysical universe. You would never be bored either. And yet even here—with a stable memory, consistent desires, and a continuously novel flow of life events—there'd be a problem with living forever. Sooner or later you would come to feel profoundly antiquated. You'd feel haunted by your memories of bygone days and mired in your old-fashioned desires and values, while the world hurtled on in directions you wouldn't understand or appreciate. You'd become terminally nostalgic.

The only remaining immortality scenario would seem to be one in which your memories periodically disappeared to be superseded by entirely new ones, and your desires and values repeatedly fell away over time to be supplanted by wholly unrelated ones, and yet not much that's new actually ever happened to you. But how enviable would that kind of unending life be? Its closest cousin in mortal life—unstable memory, inconstant desires, rigidly repetitive flow of life events—seems to be a kind of dementia.

Maybe, these various braided strands of thought suggest, immortality would be nothing but a kind of box. No matter where they looked, immortal humans would ultimately face a wall: crushing boredom, multiple serial personalities, bitter nostalgia, futile dementia. Perhaps, then, we mortals in fact have it pretty good: as good as it could ever get. And that's some consolation.

A fourth and final consolatory stream takes yet a different tack. It reminds us that the principal evils we associate with being dead routinely happen to us in life anyway. Within life—this vale of tears—we already face everything that we dread about death. In fact *life, with its losses, is itself nothing but an intimation of death.* List all the evils that you think death inflicts. You will see that life, sooner or later, deals them out as well. If we were clear-eyed about this reality, then death would cease to be a source of terror.

Think of one of death's most stinging deprivations: our having to part forever from the people and things we love. This happens in life all the time anyway. "Husbands walk out, wives walk out," says Joan Didion.[3] We lose cherished jobs, beloved homes, treasured keepsakes, life-sustaining ideals and convictions all the time. Goodbyes are endemic to life, with every turn in the wheel of fortune, just as much as they are to death: so says the fourth consolation for our mortal condition.

Of course, there's one goodbye that death specializes in and that life seems unable to intimate: the goodbye to our own individual consciousness itself, not simply to all of the people and pursuits and places and possessions that populate it. And yet not only does life, too, contain its own periods when we bid adieu to our consciousness—hence the reference to death as the "big sleep," which I will discuss—but it threatens something more. Consider the visionaries who have recently led the fight against death, such as Ray Kurzweil, Marvin Minsky, and Hans Moravec. At some point, they say, human life will become "post-human." By uploading our minds onto supercomputers we will "merge" or "meld" into a single, eternal, universal consciousness of immense power, opening up dazzling insights into hidden patterns of the cosmos that at present remain beyond our ken.

Let's suppose that what these futurists sketchily foresee does come to pass. Isn't what they herald not so much a form of immortality as it is the final frontier in life's intimation of death's losses? After all, individual consciousness—what it is we most value in life—would eventually perish in (post)human life, with its single universal consciousness, every bit as much as it does now with death. It's just that what disappears would be the "individual" part, not the "consciousness" part. Perhaps we are deeply fortunate to be living mortals now, in the early twenty-first century, before the posthuman era commences. And that's some consolation.

*

Death is benign. Mortality gives us all the goods that immortality would. Immortality would be malignant. Life gives us all the bads that death does.

In the pages that follow, I explore these four broad consolations, and the different flavors in which each of them comes. My overriding question is this: Can one or more or all or none of them—or perhaps something else altogether—really and truly reconcile us, we early twenty-first-century bundles of ego and anxiety who love life, to our mortality?

A few words about some red herrings. One purported consolation for mortality is that we should welcome death because it puts an agreeable end to the degradations of aging—macular degeneration, arthritis, Parkinson's, Alzheimer's. I don't buy this argument. After all, the reverse claim almost as often gets made: that we should welcome the degradations of aging—macular degeneration, arthritis, and so on—because they make death, which rescues us from them, easier to take, even seem like a blessing. Montaigne, who otherwise had brilliant insights to offer on the topic of mortality, said both of these things. But their circularity suggests that we'd simply be better off without either: without the death that ends the awful degradation, without the degradation that eases us toward accepting terrible death.

So my assumption, throughout, is that we are talking about whether mortality is a good or a bad thing for people who otherwise remain healthy. That of course is the toughest case. And we must bear in mind that medical science might continue extending the span over which most of us are able to remain well. True, for a separate set of reasons—population growth, strains on resources, the choking-off of opportunities—the fact that even the healthy aged die might be a good thing for the human species as a whole. But I am concerned here with whether mortality can be a good thing for the healthy person herself who dies.

Also: by a mortal life, I mean one that extends to whatever the normal human span happens to be at any point in time. I don't discuss the merits of mortality when it falls short of a normal span. No one, in our era when a normal life span is approximately eighty, can say a good word about the premature death of an otherwise healthy and flourishing person, say a cancer victim in her twenties, or a six-year-old who is struck by a car and killed.

Nor do I discuss the merits of increased longevity, an increase in the normal life span, short of immortality. If a life span of eighty years is good, it's hard to see why a life span of ninety or one hundred, or perhaps two hundred or two thousand or even twenty thousand or two hundred thousand years should necessarily be bad. I don't know where the border between increased longevity and for-all-intents-and-purposes immortality can be found. As the geneticist Francis Collins says, "One man's longevity is another man's immortality."[4]

An immortal life doesn't literally have to be endless. But it must feel, to those living it, as if it were endless—and not simply a mortal life of vastly increased longevity.

This book, then, pits mortality against immortality while taking no position on how much longevity has to increase before mortality becomes immortality. Put another way, wherever one draws the line between an effectively mortal and an effectively immortal life, the consolations, based as they are simply on the ideas of mortality and immortality, will have the same relevance.

Finally, I will look widely at works of philosophy and literature, as well as at popular culture: film, sports, music, letters, memorial plaques, bucket lists, the musings of celebrities, and more. I come to them as someone with a question that's been dogging me—whether I can reconcile myself to my mortality—searching our collective literary, philosophical, and cultural wisdom for insights that will help me find an answer. And I do so precisely from the perspective not of a philosopher or a literary critic, but of an everyday bundle of ego and anxieties who loves life and is looking to console himself about death. This book is written for those who might be on the same quest. And it offers a way of thinking about—a critical guide to—the main ideas on offer.

One last thing. I promised myself, when I began this project, that I would write the most upbeat book that I honestly could. I have kept that promise.

PART 1

Death Is Benign

one

ATTENDING YOUR OWN FUNERAL

Chulkaturin, the dying "hero" of Turgenev's *Diary of a Superfluous Man*, believes that his life has left no mark on the world. He feels like a fifth wheel on a four-wheel cart. The lives of others, and events in general, would have rolled along in much the same way even if he had never existed.

But this is puzzling. For as Turgenev tells it, Chulkaturin collides spectacularly with other people, leaving their lives indelibly different. He spends hours, days, weeks in the presence of the woman he loves, Liza, alternatively garrulous and glum without ever pressing his suit, continually exasperating and finally alienating her. Upset with his own dallying, he then provokes a duel with the visiting prince who wins Liza's heart, wounding him and this time antagonizing the entire community. Chulkaturin might be cowardly and conflicted, and he might have anger management issues. But his life doesn't seem superfluous, like a fifth wheel on a four-wheel cart. It seems more like a reckless, careening cart itself, leaving a permanent mark on the world and everyone around him.

Chulkaturin records these events in his diary as he lies dying of a fatal illness, and his deathbed perspective is key here. He finds himself, even in these final days, languorously dragging his pen across the page much as he had lived his life, "without haste . . . as though I still had years ahead of me": as if death were nothing to him. That's why Liza slipped through his fingers. Never grabbing the moment with her, never bringing matters to a head—he thought he had all the time in the world—he awakens one morning to find Liza betrothed to another man. Not, as it happens, the prince (who has spurned her) but the local official Biz'menkov. "Biz'menkov had probably said to Liza exactly what I was going to say to her," Chulkaturin thinks to himself self-torturously, and "she had given him the answer I longed to hear from her."[1]

It is as if Biz'menkov had unhorsed Chulkaturin from the saddle of his own life, and Chulkaturin then had to stand on the sidelines and watch that life galloping on ahead without him. In fact, ever since he can remember, Chulkaturin has always felt this way: "Throughout my entire life, I have found that my spot [in it] was taken."[2] And herein lies Chulkaturin's superfluousness. It's not that his own life has been irrelevant to the lives of others. It's that he, Chulkaturin, has somehow become irrelevant to his own life. Because he had banished death from his mind he dawdled and tarried, never seizing the reins himself. Now, as he is about to die, it seems to him that his life is going to continue on very nicely in his absence, albeit under new management.

But Turgenev's Chulkaturin is not literature's—in fact not even Russian literature's—most famous superfluous man. That title goes to Tolstoy's Ivan Ilych who, although both famous and superfluous, is famous not for being superfluous but for something else. He is the most notorious death denier in all of literature. He refuses to believe that he will die. And yet Ivan's lifelong unwillingness to face his mortality is, like Chulkaturin's, intimately connected with his own superfluousness, with the sense he feels, as he approaches his untimely end, of being irrelevant to his own life.

We have, Ernest Becker famously argued in his 1973 book *The Denial of Death*, pushed death entirely out of our lives. We know on the most abstract level that we will come to an end. But we do not—and maybe could not—live our lives in the full face of that knowledge. We'd be paralyzed with fear or a sense of meaninglessness. And so we repress our awareness that extinguishment awaits us. We repress it also because it's simply impossible to imagine our no longer existing. Freud saw death denial as a fact of our individual nature: "At bottom no one believes in his own death . . . in the unconscious every one of us is convinced of his own immortality."[3] The historian Philippe Ariès, along similar lines, diagnosed death denial as a social phenomenon: consider our manner of shuttering death out of life by confining the dying to hospitals and consigning the dead to undertakers.

In other words, many of us live our lives so as to make them fertile ground for Epicurus's consolatory idea: the observation that as long as we are here death can't be and so is irrelevant to us. We know this is true as a logical proposition. But we devote ourselves to making it psychologically real for ourselves by living as if we weren't going to die—by living so that death can gain no toehold in our daily life and concerns as long as we are here.

This is what Ivan does. He thrusts his death out of his life, holds it at bay, so that it becomes as nothing to him. He exiles it to the fringes of his mind, continuously taking on new projects at work, home, and play as if he had no expiry date. A "current of thoughts," Tolstoy writes—thoughts about tonight's bridge game, his daughter's marriage potential, his getting a leg up on his rivals at work— "had always screened the thought of death from Ivan Ilych."[4] The same with many of us. Think of the busy publisher George Weidenfeld, who, in his nineties and still juggling numerous enterprises on the go, conceded that "I think about death," yet then quickly emphasized: "but I don't think it through."[5] The more projects you have to think about, the less you will think about death. And the less you think about death, the less inhibition you will feel about continuing to take on new projects.

The result is that when Ivan does die, all of those schemes, plans, and hopes—all the major pieces and parts of his life—are nowhere near ready to come to an end with him. All the continuing loose ends of his life spill over far beyond his death. But since he no longer remains alive their fate now rests in the hands of others. Ivan himself dies. But because he has been such a proficient death denier his life continues on, showing him to have become superfluous to it.

In little vignettes, Tolstoy reveals what this means. At work, the bureaucrat Alexeev, contemplating Ivan's mortal illness, daydreams that he will succeed to Ivan's seat on the Court of Justice and take over his unfinished docket of cases. At home, Ivan's friend Peter Ivanovich, paying his last respects along with a multitude of others, is damned if he's going to let Ivan's approaching demise ruin his bridge rubber that evening; the game will go on seamlessly with someone else playing Ivan's hand. Ivan's income stream too will flow on after him, in the form of a pension, except that now of course the money will be spent by his widow, Praskovya Fedorovna. Not long before Ivan dies, Praskovya Fedorovna, dressed to the nines, enters his chamber. She reminds him that, months before, they had booked a theater box to watch a Sarah Bernhardt performance that evening. But Ivan is now on his deathbed. So Praskovya Fedorovna informs him that their daughter Lisa's fiancé, Fëdor Petrishchev, will be taking Ivan's seat.

No wonder it "sometimes seemed to Ivan," as Tolstoy writes, "that people were watching him inquisitively as a man whose place might soon be vacant."[6] And there was always someone available—Alexeev, Peter Ivanovich, Praskovya Fedorovna, Fëdor Petrishchev—to take that place: to take up Ivan's own role in what would otherwise have been his own life. At court and at cards, at the marketplace and at the theater, Ivan's life will continue beyond his death. After all, by denying death any place in his life, Ivan has lived—to borrow from Ernest Becker—in a "forward momentum of activity," ever onward, never wrapping things up.[7] And so as death creeps into it, his life is still going full force, quite capable of carrying on without him. Yet although his life will survive the moment of his demise, Ivan himself, in some ways, has already predeceased it, which is why others are already assuming his place in it.

Ivan dies of internal injuries at age forty-five, a few months after a freak accident. He falls from a ladder while hanging drapes. Perhaps you can't fault Ivan (although Tolstoy does) for not thinking much about his death prior to the accident. He was, after all, a robust man in the prime of life. But his death denial persists into the period when, had he acknowledged he was dying, he could have wrapped up his life's loose ends. Had he been frank with himself about his mortality, he would have completed his major cases so that they would have been decided his way, not Alexeev's. He might have prevailed on Fëdor Petrishchev to marry Lisa while he was still on the planet. Perhaps he could have put his income in a trust, so that Praskovya Fedorovna would have spent it in accordance with his wishes, not frivolously but conserving an estate for Lisa and Fëdor Petrishchev's children. And if he had said, "I am dying," would his wife, daughter, and son-in-law-to-be have traipsed off to the theater that evening?

In fact there are two ways for Ivan to look at this reality—the reality that his life will continue on after he himself has departed. One of them is mildly comforting, the other miserably corrosive. Ironically, for all his attempts to anesthetize his mind against death's sting, Ivan chooses to look at matters in the way that, unfortunately, brings the greater amount of pain.

One evening, lying in bed as the household bustles around him as if "everything in the world was going on as usual," Ivan feels a stab of anguish. It would seem, heartbreakingly, as if he is not going to be missed at all: things will carry on very nicely without him. But then, does he feel any better on those occasions when the household comes to a full stop and his family's mournful eyes all turn to him? No. Such moments bring home to him, heartbreakingly, that he really is about to die. Each path leads to heartache. His life and its affairs will continue on without him, meaning he won't be missed, but he himself won't continue on, meaning he will miss out on them.

A shame, because there's another way to look at it. Since his life will continue on beyond him, as wife, son, and daughter suggest whenever they conduct themselves "as usual," doesn't that mean that a sizeable part of Ivan—all the cases, connubial plans, and card-game camaraderie that he commenced, that were so much a part of his life—will in fact cheat death? And shouldn't that, in some way, warm his heart? He leaves a large, continuing imprint on the world; much of what he worked on and cared about survives him. True, he himself won't elude the Reaper. But shouldn't that fact, brought home whenever wife, son, and daughter show distress, confirm how important and irreplaceable he is to them? Why not the best of both worlds—a kind of survival through the ongoing stuff of his life, while feeling that he himself will truly be missed?

But unfortunately Ivan doesn't see matters that way. He feels that he won't really, viscerally be missed so long as much of his life—his projects and pastimes, his connivings and collusions—will be able to march along without him. And yet even though much of his life will survive, he himself won't. He will die, and miss out on it all. That's how he feels. The worst of both worlds. Tolstoy's portrait—and I have looked at *Ivan Ilych* only for what it says to a nonbeliever, shorn of any of the religious messages or allegories Tolstoy intended—shows how disconsolate a life of death denial can leave a person at the end.

The denial of death leaves footprints all around us. So profoundly might we refuse to acknowledge that we will die, so expertly might we forge a life that barrels on long after we have departed, that our survivors, too, may feel compelled to deny our death—a process that Joan Didion has now irrevocably stamped with the term "magical thinking." For a year following the heart attack that killed her husband, John Gregory Dunne, many of the signs of his life continued unabated. After all, his clothes, his chair, his office were still there— much of the wake he left in the world persisted. Didion says she kept these items and spaces around because of her belief that Dunne might return—that his life was still ongoing—and he might yet need them. But the reverse is also the case. She believed his life was still ongoing because all the signs of it, its objects and spaces, persisted. There was no difference between looking into his vacant office after he had died and looking into it when he had simply gone out of town. His death was easy to deny because so much of his life seemed to persist.

If Didion's *Year of Magical Thinking* takes one view, there's a passage in another magical volume, Thomas Mann's *Magic Mountain*, that seems to take the opposing position. As soon as someone dies, Mann observes, the world almost immediately begins to seal up around the space he left. This can happen quickly. So quickly that if he were to magically return but a few days later, even those closest to him would find it disconcerting and irksome. As if a guest from last night's dinner knocked at the door the following morning to continue the revelry while we are puttering around the kitchen cleaning up.[8]

This thought might appear to jar with Didion's. For Mann, it seems as if the world heals up seamlessly around the void you leave as soon as you die, while for Didion it keeps a wide berth (your shoes, your office) open for you. But the two thoughts actually dovetail. What Didion shows is that a person's life—all its projects and pursuits as well as the infrastructure like offices and clothes that supported it—can continue on after his death. What Mann shows is how the person himself immediately disappears at, if not before, his death. If he were then somehow to return, it would seem a gauche intrusion—even into the remnants of his own life, which by now are in the custody and care of others. I used to think that the two magic books were in conflict on this point. Now I see that they are soul mates. Your life continues on after you, but almost immediately it no longer has any place for you yourself. If you were to return, you would be the skunk at your own garden party.

A final representative from literature's gallery of superfluous dying men: Willy Loman. Willy, in *Death of a Salesman*, persuades himself that for his life to continue—for all his projects and pursuits to be realized, his sons Biff and Happy to succeed, his wife, Linda, to enjoy a stable income, his mortgage to be paid—he has only to remove himself from that life. He simply has to kill himself—kill himself in a car "accident" so that his insurance will provide his loved ones with an annuity. Willy's choice isn't "your money or your life." It's your "self or your life (with money)."

Willy is a death denier. Till the very last, he is still planting seeds whose saplings he will never see. Yes, he knows he is about to kill himself, he knows it's "late." But even so he can't wrap his life up. Instead he keeps, so to speak, his pedal to the metal as if it were business as usual right up till the end. He gives no thought to that end itself, he has nothing to say about his death even as it looms. As long as he is here, his death remains out of view, and he continues to plunge furiously into the ongoing business of his life.

And in a way he succeeds. His life does survive him, his projects are realized. The final payment on the mortgage gets made. Linda now has a secure pension; there is a stake for Biff. And with Willy out of the picture, the boys no longer have any reason to stay away from

Linda or each other, thus healing the family unit. His life forges on so robustly in his absence that Linda, at the funeral, finds it difficult to shed a tear. "Forgive me, dear. I can't cry. I don't know what it is, but I can't cry. . . . It seems to me that you're just on another trip. I keep expecting you. Willy, dear, I can't cry."

Willy does, though, achieve something more, something that Ivan Ilych does not. One of Willy's happiest moments comes earlier in the play when, as he imagines himself talking to his brother Ben, he fantasizes about his own funeral: "Ben," Willy rhapsodizes, "that funeral will be massive! They'll come from Maine, Massachusetts, Vermont, New Hampshire! . . . [Biff will] see what I am, Ben! He's in for a shock, that boy!"[9]

What purpose does this bit of magical thinking serve for Willy? Well, two things perhaps. First, Willy rapturously imagines his life being eulogized, elegized, capped—wrapped up. All the wonderful things they will say about him, what a fitting conclusion, what a high note to end the story on. Second, although his life is wrapped up, Willy himself still manages to be there, as we all must imagine ourselves to be whenever we visualize our own funerals, observing the ceremony from some floating vantage point in the air. His life is done, marked, and missed. Yet he himself somehow still survives, continuing on to enjoy the adulation and acclamation. The best of both worlds.

This is just a wish. Perhaps it's a wish to which death deniers, as we all are to some degree, are particularly prone. But the reality is just the other way around. It is Willy himself who's gone, while his life continues to soldier on as if he himself had long since ceased to be relevant to it. And just for that reason, he himself will not be missed—not deeply, not in the gut. Because his life so resoundingly marches on, his absence is hard to get a handle on, to viscerally feel. And so Linda can't cry.[10]

Hey, I'm Not Done Yet

As long as we are here, death isn't. And then as soon as death comes, we are no longer here to be harmed by it. As logical propositions, the two sentences in Epicurus's consolation for mortality are hard to deny. They also seem utterly consistent with each other. No daylight appears between them. And yet as Epicurus realized, and as contemporary philosophers who debate them as metaphysical propositions recognize, though logically compelling they are far from psychologically gripping. And so they fall far short of consoling us.

We can, though, take measures to render them more psychologically convincing. There are ways, as I will suggest, of trying to live our lives so as to make Epicurus's two sentences more like meaningful realities than arid truisms. But a funny thing then happens. The kind of life we would have to lead to make the first of Epicurus's sentences psychologically persuasive—as long as we are here, death won't yet have come and so cannot harm us—conflicts, profoundly, with the kind of life we would have to lead to gain any kind of psychological comfort from the second: as soon as death does come, we will have departed and so no longer remain present to be hurt by it. The more the two phrases stand a chance of consoling us at least to some extent, the less coherent they become. As they grow more deeply psychological and less purely logical, they become less consistent and more mutually contradictory.

To grasp this, consider Epicurus's first sentence, which I will from now on call "Epicurus's first consolation": as long as we are here, our death cannot be. This is undeniable as a dry, objective assertion. But if we want to make it a vibrant subjective reality, we must (as many of us do to some degree) lead an Ivan Ilych kind of life, taking on new cases, making new plans for our children, daring our friends to top our latest score in cards—or engaging in fresh romantic adventures, embarking on new political campaigns, training for ever more strenuous bike races—and engross ourselves in all of these activities to such a degree that our death becomes but a faint, indistinct glimmer on the outer edges of our mind. Because we are so very much present, death gets pushed aside, totally out of the picture. It becomes psychologically and not just logically absent for as long as we are here.

But there's an irony. Yes, we will have lived so as to make Epicurus's first consolation—as long as we are here, death isn't—as psychologically real for ourselves as it can be. But in doing so we will have made Epicurus's second consolation—once death does arrive, we will no longer be here to be hurt by it—about as psychologically remote as it can be. Think of Ivan. For as long as he is here death is never present—never present to him subjectively, in his thoughts, let alone objectively, as a fact. And so he never gives any consideration to wrapping things up in advance of his demise. The result? Large parts of himself—all the objective parts, the facts in the world that constitute the raw material of his life such as important legal files and betrothals and card matches—will still very much be here, ongoing even after death comes. And it hurts him deeply to think that other parts of himself—his subjective consciousness, his cognitive and emotional capacities—won't any longer be present to relish or cherish or pursue those cases and weddings and games.[11]

In this psychological sense, then, it's not true—as Epicurus's second consolation would have it—that once death comes, there is nothing of Ivan left and hence that he can't be harmed. And that's precisely because Ivan has lived his life so as to take maximum advantage of Epicurus's first consolation: that as long as he was around, there was going to be no hint of death.

So what about Epicurus's second consolation? What kind of life would we have to live in order to find ourselves maximally consoled by the idea that once death comes, we will no longer be here to be harmed by it? Certainly not Ivan's.

We wouldn't continually start new endeavors and embark on new projects, as Ivan does, with the risk that our life will continue on without us, long after death ushers our selves out of the picture, depriving us of the capacity to guide and enjoy it. Instead, we'd try to be fast out of the gate. We'd get all our endeavors and projects completed in a hurry, wrapping our life up as soon as possible long before we ourselves take our leave. We'd lobby to get the biggest cases we could try over and done with. We'd push our daughter to marry early. We'd establish a record of uninterrupted card-game victories that no one in our circle could ever match. That way, death would be powerless to harm us by cutting short our plans or taking us from projects that are half-completed. Instead, we'd live according to the principle Holderlin invoked in his poem "To the Fates": "A single summer grant me . . . and a single autumn for fully ripened song . . . once what I am bent on, my poetry, is accomplished, [b]e welcome then, stillness of the shadows' world!"

If we adopted what the philosopher Ben Bradley calls the "Holderlin strategy," we would make a big success of ourselves as early in our lives as we could.[12] We'd get our accomplishments—professional triumphs, romantic affairs, lyric poetry, military glory, hiking to the top of Everest, biking the Tour de France, whatever—engraved on the record. Then we would relax and enjoy the world's simple pleasures—such as eating, drinking, and making love—that are not graven on the record but that disappear with each day's sunset, creating the need for them anew. We'd know that death can never destroy the more "important" stuff, the accomplishments that have now moved safely into the past, preserved in amber for us to reflect upon with a secure smile on our faces. And we'd know too that the daily setting of the sun—in other words, life itself—regularly washes away the other stuff, the pleasure of sex or the satisfaction of hunger, so that the only way to quench our need for them permanently would be to die. We'd thus ease into a mindset accepting of death.

If we lived this way, then Epicurus's second consolation—once our death comes, we ourselves will no longer be present to be affected by it—would not simply be a dry logical truism. More important to our psychic well-being, long before our death comes, the life we wanted to lead would be over and done with, invulnerable now to the Reaper whenever he might appear. Any number of people live a life that follows this pattern. Some are able to get it done very early: Björn Borg sought to put it all behind him—five consecutive Wimbledon championships—by retiring at twenty-six. Philip Roth called it a day much later, giving up writing at eighty and becoming "the only living novelist to have his work published in a comprehensive, definitive edition by the Library of America."[13] Like the writer Clive James, those who seek to ensure that their lives are over before death rears its head tend to talk of themselves—and certainly their lives—in the past tense: "I didn't get a bad ride," James says; "I managed to square the circle."[14]

Suppose that we follow this kind of path. We might well reap the psychic advantages of Epicurus's second consolation—that when death comes, neither we *nor* our lives will still be here to be harmed by it. But there'd be a cost. We would then live in a way that flouts Epicurus's first consolation, according to which as long as we are here, death can have no contact with us and so is nothing to us. For in fact death would be constantly present. Not as an objective reality of course. But subjectively, in our psyche.

When I read the memoirs or biographies of individuals who have set their lives in granite, making psychologically real to themselves Epicurus's second consolation—once death comes, nothing of their lives can any longer be harmed by it—they seem, like Henry Kissinger, for example, as if they are dearly seeking the chance to experience their own posthumous glory. They want to know firsthand what it would be like to look back on their own lives once they're over. They aspire to live in a kind of death zone that they can experience for themselves—one with all the tranquility and other good things they associate with death but without the actual reality—by retiring at their peak and then reflecting on and burnishing their own success.

But in so doing they precisely *want* it to be the case that even while they remain here among the living, their death has in a sense already happened—contrary to the spirit of Epicurus's first consolation: as long as we are here, death cannot be. Perhaps that's why Björn Borg, as he approached the end of his tennis career, looked as if he were already wearing a "death mask."[15]

"In the coming years, I have two great calamities to face, death and biography," Philip Roth says. "Let's hope the first comes first."[16] But in fact it already has. Roth is famously aware of death. In fact, he invited death into the center of his mind from the outer reaches decades ago. And so he ended his life at eighty, giving himself some time to enjoy it posthumously before he himself departs. His life completed, Roth can now help write its complete story—his own biography. He's collaborating on it.

Let me return now to the kind of life we would have to lead to make Epicurus's first consolation—as long as we are here, death can't be—as psychologically real to ourselves as we possibly could. What, really, do we have to do to banish death so convincingly from our concerns that it becomes a benign irrelevancy? I will turn to Epicurus's second consolation in the next chapter.

The Late Me

In 2006, the NYU philosopher J. David Velleman delivered a charming lecture at Amherst College called "So It Goes." It's the most penetrating account I have seen of the life we must lead if Epicurus's first consolation—that as long as we are here, death can't be and so is truly irrelevant to us—is to take full psychological hold.[17]

Suppose, Velleman says, that you likened the relationship between your "self" and "time" to the relationship between your body and space. Imagine your body standing up in a particular space—say your living room. Even though your head is closer than your feet to the ceiling, you would never say that your body itself moves closer and closer to the ceiling over the space from your feet to your head. Likewise: even though your eighties are closer to your death than your twenties, there's no reason to think that you yourself move closer and closer to your death over the course of time from your twenties to your eighties.

What exactly does this mean? To begin with, we must understand that Velleman offers this unconventional image in order to challenge a more conventional one: that you are a self who, much like a jogger, runs the course of your life over time from birth to death, with different parts of that course coming into view as you chug along. If that's how you see things then obviously, as you travel the road of your life, you yourself, the jogger, will get closer and closer to death. Death will loom larger and larger on the horizon, creeping ever more menacingly into view, thus deflating any kind of consolation that rests on the idea that as long as you are here, death isn't and so is an irrelevancy.

On this conventional image, then, your life is stretched out in time much as a road stretches out in space. And you—your self, the runner—are pacing through it. What Velleman suggests, in effect, is that you should instead view your self as extended out in time in exactly the way your life is: that you conceive of the two, your self and your life, as stretched out side by side. The part of your self that exists on April 23, 2014, from 4 to 5 PM enjoys the part of your life that's unfolding on April 23, 2014, from 4 to 5 PM—say the coffee you're sharing with a friend. Then a different and subsequent part of your self—the part that exists on April 23, 2014, from 5 to 6 PM— savors the next part of your life, the ride home you are giving your six-year-old daughter. Each part of your self lives only in its own moment of your life.

On Velleman's unconventional image, then, there never is a "you" —there never is a whole, entire self—that is moving moment by moment toward death over time. There are only different parts of you at different times. After all, there is no "you" moving inch by inch toward the ceiling in space either. There are only different parts of you—knees, stomach, shoulders—at different heights. No reason, then, for you to think of death as something to which *you* steadily grow nearer, any more than the ceiling is something to which *you* steadily grow closer. You can fully avail yourself of Epicurus's first consolation: as long as any part of your self is here, death is utterly irrelevant. Not only is it not present. *You* are not even moving toward it.[18]

Sleight of hand? Velleman's perspective, and similar "perdurantist" views, makes some other philosophers uneasy. D. H. Mellor captures the nub of the issue. Churchill wrote a book called *My Early Life*, Mellor notes. He did not title it "Early Me."[19] "I" myself do not come in different parts, earlier ones and then later ones, in the way my life does. Instead, "I" as a whole experience each part of my life at its different points, first the earlier ones, then the later ones. Certainly, if Mellor is right—if it's not just a part of myself but my entire self that exists at 4 PM on April 23, and again at 5 PM on April 23, and so forth—then Velleman is wrong. "I" do grow closer to death as my life stretches out, because I as a whole am running through it.

Let's clear one thing up first: we might not refer to the young Churchill as the early Churchill, as Mellor suggests. But we certainly would at one point have referred to the dead Churchill as the late Churchill. Why so?

Whatever the historical origins of this usage of "late"—and they remain unclear—here is a contemporary interpretation. "Late" means two things. First, it means tardy. If someone is late, it generally means that he is not here yet, although he was expected to be. And that might be just how we feel about someone who has died. Like Joan Didion, we might have the persisting sense that he is merely delayed out of town but on his way, not actually dead. He's late.

But of course, this sense of "late" works for a deceased person only if he has died recently. It makes less and less sense to say—or feel—that we are expecting a dead person to arrive, that he is simply tardy, as time passes. And this is where the second meaning of "late" comes in: as a synonym not for "tardy" but for "recent," as in, "It's been raining around here of late." While we might have used the phrase "the late Churchill" in the year following Churchill's 1965 death, when he had only recently died—when we could still say that he was here of late—we wouldn't anymore. So the two senses of "late"—not yet here (tardy) but expected to be; was just here (recently) though is no longer—infuse one another in a kind of double image. We think only of the recently dead as tardy, of the lately dead as late. Perhaps that's why we save the word "late" just for them.

For Velleman, though, just because it sounds strange doesn't mean it's mistaken to talk of an "early me"—an early part of myself—that experiences my early life. Or of another part of myself—"mid me"—

that experiences my midlife. Or of still another part—"late me"—
that experiences my late life. What would no longer make sense, if we
were remaining faithful to Velleman's imagery, would be to call the
early part of my self my "younger self," or the mid part my "middle-
aged self," or the later part my "older self." That would imply that my
self as a whole gets older, it's been around longer, as time passes. But
in fact any *part* of my self that comes into existence later in life—and
of course for Velleman a part is all that exists at any given time—is no
older, it's not been around for any longer, than any other part of my
self ever is. The part of my self that exists from 10 to 11 AM on January 29, 2015, doesn't grow any older than did the part that existed fifteen years earlier, from 10 to 11 AM on January 29, 2000. Nor does
that later part grow any closer to death during its existence than does
the earlier part. As Montaigne asks, "Why are you afraid of your last
day? It brings you no closer to your death than any other did."[20]

What does this have to do with Epicurus's first consolation? Suppose, Velleman says, that we accept with Epicurus that as long as we
are here in any way, shape, or form, death must remain offstage—
and so in that sense is nothing to us. Even so, Velleman says, it would
still make sense for us to feel "anxiety about [our] inexorable *approach*
to death": the fact that our terminus looms ever larger on the horizon, that we are ineluctably, moment by moment, approaching our
end—even if, in the final moment, we will disappear just as death
arrives and so won't actually encounter it.[21] We could banish *that*
anxiety, and thus truly feel that death is nothing to us for as long as
we're here, only if we no longer saw ourselves as moving forward in
time toward it. And so to fully access Epicurus's first consolation,
Velleman concludes, we must buy into the particular analogy he offers. Our self, in fact, doesn't move forward in time at all. It simply
stretches out over time, its different parts occupying their own different moments. In just the same way our body, say, or a statue, doesn't
move ever upward over space. It simply stretches out over space, its
different parts occupying their own different places.

It's a stimulating if somewhat mind-bending idea. But it poses a puzzle. Very few of us look at our selves in the way Velleman recommends. And yet most of us happen to be quite adept at forgetting—at shutting out of our minds—the fact that we are drawing closer to death moment by moment. We do manage to treat our finitude as an irrelevancy in our day-to-day life. We rarely operate as if death bulked ever larger on the horizon with the passing of each day. Most of us are Ivans to some extent. How do we accomplish that?

The surprising answer: precisely because, contrary to Velleman, we do not—in fact we cannot—treat our self's relationship to time as if it were like a body's relationship to space.

Think of the image of the self that Velleman rejects: our self running the race course of our life such that death looms ever larger in front of us. It's true that when we are running a real race course, a distant object—say a mountain on the far horizon—does grow ever larger in our view. Our eyes give us a sense that we are getting closer to distant spatial objects, via their increasing size and clarity, as we approach them. Our mind's eye, however, fails to give us a similar sense that we are getting closer to distant temporal events, including our death, as we approach them. We don't, in our minds, experience future events—we don't visualize them—as becoming progressively larger and clearer over time as we draw nearer to them.[22] And so death deniers like Ivan find it easy to conclude, along the lines of Epicurus's first consolation, that death has nothing to do with them. Their imagination—that flawed faculty—doesn't convey a real and vibrant sense of death looming progressively bigger and sharper even as they jog toward it. Until perhaps, as for Ivan, it is right in front of them.

It's helpful to couple this observation with another one, about events not in the future but in the past. When we look back at a particular event from time gone by, we don't see the intervening years. A memorable incident from long ago can thus feel (as we often say) as if it happened yesterday, as if not much in the way of time has intermediated. By contrast, we would never say of an object at a long distance behind us in space that it's "as if it were right next to us." We retain a full perceptual sense of all the terrain that intervenes. Distant events in our temporal rearview mirror, however, often appear closer than they are, the past shorter than it is. Our memories fail to give us a sense of the decades in between. And so as we move through our life, the time we have put behind us can continue to *feel* shorter than the time that still remains—until, perhaps, death is right in front of us.

As we run the temporal "race course" of our lives, then, our flawed imaginations make the end of the journey seem perpetually farther away than it is. And our gappy memories make the beginning seem consistently nearer than it is. We thus find it easy, like Ivan, to deny our movement forward in time from birth to death. When we run a spatial race course, by contrast, the end of the journey appears perpetually nearer and the beginning consistently farther away.

We could make death irrelevant, Velleman says. All we have to do is deeply, truly come to see that no more does our self move through time toward death than our body moves through space toward the ceiling. But most of us already make death irrelevant. And we do so precisely because we *fail* to perceive our self moving through time toward death in the way we perceive our body moving through space toward the horizon.

Day to day, our memories and imaginations conspire to muffle our sense that we are moving ever forward in time toward death. That muffling is quite effective—so much so that we aren't totally desperate for a radical alternative like Velleman's. But the sense we have of ourselves moving ever forward in time toward our ends is also, finally, deeply ingrained; we couldn't embrace a radical alternative like Velleman's even if we wanted to.

We can't view our self as stationary in time in the way an object—a statue, say—might be stationary in space. We simply aren't, as Velleman himself at one point acknowledges, psychologically wired to do so, certainly not we early twenty-first-century bundles of ego and anxiety. Day to day we might be Ivans, "little busy bee[s]," as Edmund White says. Yet at three in the morning, in the proverbial "dark night of the soul," we know we are relentlessly moving toward our end.[23] For most of us, Epicurus's first consolation, on which as long as we are here death isn't, will finally have little psychological purchase.[24]

two

The two consolations embodied in Epicurus's famous observation—as long as we are here death can't be, and once death does come we are no longer here—seem logically tight with each other. But, as we have seen, they conflict as recommendations for living our life.

Consider: to take full advantage of Epicurus's second consolation—once death comes, we will no longer be here to be harmed by it—we must hasten to wrap our life up before the Reaper comes. The goal would be to leave him no hostages, to live according to the "Holderlin strategy." Recall, from the previous chapter, Holderlin's plea: a "single summer grant me . . . once . . . my poetry is accomplished, [b]e welcome then, stillness of the shadows' world!" Once our accomplishments are done, nothing—not even death—can take them away. Epicurus's second consolation, which I consider in this chapter, will then have maximal force. Death will arrive, only to find that not just we, but our lives too, are no longer present to be harmed by it. But the price, for anyone who follows the Holderlin strategy, is that Epicurus's first consolation—as long as we are here, death can't be—is no longer psychologically available.

Why not? Well, consider Jason Miller's 1972 play *That Championship Season*. A high-school basketball coach brandishes a trophy to his winning team at their twenty-year reunion: "See the names engraved on it!" Coach bellows at the men. "I carved your names in silver, last forever, forever, never forget that."[1] The greatest moment in the men's lives—in fact, their lives themselves—finished twenty years earlier. There's nothing anymore of importance for death to interrupt. Even the Reaper can't expunge the names carved in the trophy. As Seneca said, their kind of life "can neither be troubled nor snatched away," even by death. It is an "everlasting and unanxious possession." The teammates have total access to Epicurus's second consolation: when death comes, not only they—but their lives—will no longer be there to be harmed by it.

And yet precisely for this reason, Epicurus's first consolation—as long as they are here, death can't be—becomes totally inaccessible to them. For even though their selves are still here, in a crucial sense they have already died. One team member, George, reflecting that his life ended with its high-water mark of twenty years earlier, laments: "Everything is in the past tense. I'm in the past tense."[2] His life is now over, even though he himself still has decades to go. And so it seems to George, contrary to Epicurus's first consolation, as if death has already arrived while he himself is still here. In fact, ever since his life ended, his existence has in a way been a posthumous one.

The Holderlin strategy—the strategy that makes real Epicurus's second consolation, by ensuring that once death arrives our life is long over and can't be harmed by it—thus poses a dilemma. It's one that the thirtyish actor Jonah Hill once nicely illustrated. Reflecting on his life over a beer with the *New Yorker* writer Tad Friend, Hill mused: "My twenties were one hundred per cent about work. My excess was moviemaking—I made over thirty films. Now I want to focus on being around, physically present, for the possibility of re-lationships to happen—marriage, kids." Sounds like the Holderlin strategy—except Hill then immediately anticipates the downside: "I mean, it's not *over*, it was great, it is great, it will still be great. I don't know what the hell I'm talking about. Cheers!"[3]

In this chapter, I look at the challenges faced by those who follow the Holderlin strategy, those who seek to live a life that ends before (sometimes long before) they themselves do, a life set in amber so that death cannot touch it. They live so as to gain maximum psy-chological connection to Epicurus's second consolation: once death comes, we are no longer here to be harmed by it. Their goal is to achieve as early on in life as possible, and then relax for the remain-der. But as Jonah Hill realizes, it's not easy to rest on your laurels, because it involves living in a kind of death zone while you're still here—contrary to the spirit of Epicurus's first consolation.

But before looking at the relationship between a happy life and one where the high peak of achievement comes at the beginning, let's examine the relationship between a happy life and one where the high peak of achievement comes at the end.

Call No Man Happy Until He Is Dead

"Call no man happy until he is dead," the statesman Solon is said to have warned King Croesus. At the time, the king was knee-deep in "gold and silver and many precious stones," Tolstoy tells us in his story *Croesus and Fate*, "as well as numberless soldiers and slaves."[4] Not surprisingly, for most of his forty-eight years Croesus "thought that in all the world there could be no happier man than himself." But Solon was right. After remaining happy for a very long stretch, Croesus entered a bad endgame. His son lost his life in an accident. His wife committed suicide. And he himself spent his final days in humiliating captivity. If we accept Solon's dictum, then we can't call Croesus happy after all. No matter how good your life may have been, if it ended badly, that's what counts.

Millennia later, the jazz musician Scatman John led a hardscrabble life until well into his fifties, when he released a song that went to number one. "Ski-Ba-Bop-Ba-Dop-Bop" rocketed the Scatman to fame a few scant years before he died at fifty-seven. Even though he had endured a life of overall hardship, he enjoyed a brilliant if short endgame. So if we accept Solon's dictum we can call Scatman John happy. True?

The question here pits quantity against finality. Is it better to have had a much greater quantity of happiness than unhappiness over the course of one's life, even though the ending was unhappy—or to have had a happy ending, even if there was a lot more unhappiness than happiness in one's life as a whole? If we have to choose, is cumulative happiness more to be coveted than "culminative" happiness? Or is it the other way around?

Neither. The dichotomy between culmination and cumulation is, at least in the most important respect, an illusion.

Think of a football game, the Lions versus the Rams. Scoring more points than the Rams in each of the game's first three quarters, the Lions go into the final fifteen minutes ahead, 30–5. The Rams then dominate the final quarter, scoring ten unanswered points. Even though things got better for the Rams in the final stretch, and things worse for the Lions, it's still the Lions who win in the end, 30–15. That's because once a point has been scored, it becomes part of the cumulation; it never disappears. Even if the Lions had scored all of their thirty points in the first quarter, those points would have stuck around to dominate at the end. The one who scored more points, cumulatively, is also the one who's on top in the end, culminatively. In this sense there's no dichotomy between quantity and finality. We would say that the Lions didn't end the game happy—even if they dominated the first three quarters—only if, in the final quarter, the Rams scored so much more that they then won the game. But in that case the Lions not only would have culminated badly, they would have had the lower cumulation as well. Finality still matches quantity; there's no dichotomy.

When someone—take Scatman John—ends a life of obscurity with a short period of spectacular recognition, he will often say that it made up for all the years of hardship. What he is saying is that not only did his life have a happy ending, but it did so because the final period was so happy that, in quantitative terms, it outweighed all the previous unhappiness. Culminatively his life ended happy because, cumulatively, total happiness surpassed total unhappiness. As he was dying, Scatman John declared, "Whatever God wants is fine by me . . . I've had the very best life."[5]

But matters were different for the writer Michael Morpurgo. For the first time, at age sixty-four, Morpurgo had a theatrical success with the play *War Horse*, based on a little-noticed novel he'd written years earlier. That vindication was not, however, enough for him to pronounce his life happy. "It has changed my life enormously,"

Morpurgo declared, "but at the wrong end. I'm nearly 70. I'm flattered, but I'm also slightly vexed that it's the same book that's been out there for 30 years." Morpurgo's late life was better—in fact, "enormously" better—than what had gone on up till that point. But not, cumulatively, by enough so that he was prepared to say, culminatively, that it was likely to end on a happy note: he felt he was still in the red, not fully redeemed.[6] If the cumulation of happiness is insufficient, then the culmination won't be happy either, even if things get considerably happier at the end.[7]

"No man ever served the Crown in so many and such important posts as the subject of this biography," the *Saturday Review* of March 4, 1905, declared in discussing a new book about the illustrious Marquis of Dufferin and Ava.[8] The Marquis was by turns Chancellor of the Duchy of Lancaster, Under-Secretary of State for War, Governor General of Canada, and, ultimately, Viceroy of all of India. He held a KP, a GCB, a GCSI, a GCMG, a GCIE, and a PC. And yet in the final analysis the reviewer, too, felt compelled to invoke Solon: "Call no man happy until he is dead." Why so? Perhaps it's because, as the review's last line tells us, the Marquis, "like many another, died babbling of the playing fields of Eton."

Not a great ending, true—babbling of Eton after having been a baron of the empire. But then as Thomas Nagel points out, in that sense a "bad end is in store for us all."[9] And yet many of us—despite the difficult and debilitated ending that awaits—would say nonetheless that we should be called happy when we die, as long as we are happy about our life as a whole. Surely, then, Dufferin and Ava's prodigious accomplishments outweighed, in a cumulative sense, a little babbling at the end. And so wouldn't he, in a culminative sense, have led a happy life? Why the reference to Solon?

Not because of the final month or so of babbling. Rather, following his long string of triumphs, the Marquis was involved in a sensational financial scandal that left the mining firm he had chaired bankrupt and blotted out all the wonderful things he had done. He didn't die happy, but not because he was blubbering at the very end. He didn't die happy because in his life, taken as a whole, the sharpness of the grief outweighed the smugness of the gratification. The ending was determined by what happened in toto, not simply by what happened at the end itself.

So when Solon says, "Call no man happy until he is dead," what is the best way to understand him? Is it that you have to wait until the final period to determine whether the overall happiness in your life outweighs the unhappiness? Or is it that you have to wait till the final period to determine whether the final period is unhappy—on the grounds that if it is, your life will end unhappily no matter how much good preceded it? The former makes more sense: and so any dichotomy between cumulative happiness over the duration of one's life and culminative happiness late in life is a false one.

Has-beens

So let's turn now to another dichotomy, a real one: continuing to stay in the arena to cumulate successes over the duration of one's life versus going for colossal success early in life and then relaxing. Going for early successes is what the Holderlin strategy recommends. That way, you maximize your psychological access to Epicurus's second consolation: once death comes, there will be nothing left of your life for it to harm or despoil.

Say you played on a storied basketball team near the beginning of your life, as did the men of Jason Miller's play. You won the state high-school championship with a turnaround jump shot in the last five seconds, the stuff of barroom and billiard-hall legend ever since. Or, to take another example, early on you won the title of Miss America. Should you listen to Holderlin, and decide that "more isn't necessary"? There's an advantage and a disadvantage to the "Holderlin strategy," the strategy of getting life's accomplishments done early, replacing—as soon as possible—a continuously gnawing anxiety about whether you'll ever make it with the secure knowledge that in fact you did.

The advantage: once you've won a basketball championship, or a Miss America title, no one can take that victory away from you. It's emblazoned in the history books. It's on the record. You can relax for the remainder of your years—at least about your life. As Third Eye Blind rocker Stephen Jenkins puts it, "The Clash, The Police, Led Zeppelin—they all had their moment [on top of the charts], but it's locked in time."[10] Death comes too late to take it away.

The disadvantage: once a new season starts, your championship in the previous season begins sinking into history, receding further and further into the past. Unlike boxing, where the champion can hold his title for as long as he remains undefeated, in high-school basketball, say, or in beauty contests, the champions automatically lose the title the following season without being defeated. Last year's Miss America gives up the crown to this year's without losing the contest to her. Likewise the members of last year's victorious senior high-school basketball team. That championship season is immune to their death, but not to the passage of time.

Other socially recognized triumphs, however, do not get set in amber at the cost of slipping ever further backward in time. They reverse the trade-off. They stay evergreen—they don't slip backward in time—but at the cost of remaining at risk of being wiped off the books at any moment. While commentators refer to (say) Kimberly Aiken as Miss America 1994, or simply as a former Miss America—a beauty queen can win her title only once, and then it begins fading into the past—we do not similarly refer to Tom Hanks as a former best-actor Oscar winner, nor as the Oscar-winning best actor for 1994. We simply call him an Oscar-winning best actor in the present tense. In fact, journalists often refer to Hanks not just as an Oscar-winning best actor but as a two-time Oscar-winning best actor, since he took the statue home not just in 1994 but in 1993 as well. They do this because there are no limits on the number of Oscars a person may win. You can accumulate them, tote them up, for a lifetime score, a score over the duration. The game never ends, never begins receding into history. All of Hanks's Oscars are still alive. Hanks *is* a two-time Oscar-winning best actor, top that!

But there's a price. His glory always remains tentative, never engraved in the past or set in amber but ever capable of being upset.

Unlike Kimberly Aiken, from whom no one can take away her 1994 Miss America title, two-time best-actor Hanks always has to watch his back. An ever-present threat lurks that someone else—say, Daniel Day-Lewis, who in 2013 won his third best-actor Oscar—will "top that!": will accumulate more statues. If the game or season is never over, then, in one sense, your lead in the game can always be snatched away. And you might die before you have the chance to regain it. Your triumphs are immune to the passage of time, but not to death.

No one calls Kimberly Aiken a has-been as a beauty queen. Nor would anyone say, about the men of *That Championship Season*'s high-school basketball team, that they are has-beens as basketball players. That's because they aren't in the game anymore. But a top actor who hasn't won an Oscar recently, or a professional quarterback who hasn't won a championship lately? They get called has-beens on a regular basis. That's because they're still considered to be in the game, and every occasion on which they don't win is considered a loss—as Steve Martin once made explicit when he referred to Meryl Streep's two Oscars and fifteen subsequent nominations as two wins and fifteen losses. "And on the subject of slumps," the *St. Louis Post-Dispatch* asked in 2011, "when the heck is Tom Hanks going to win another Oscar?"[11]

Kimberly Aiken had no choice. According to the social templates of achievement in the realm of physical beauty, if you want to be a glamour queen you have to adopt the Holderlin strategy. You have to play just a single season, hoping it's a glorious one as it was for her, since you can be Miss America only once, and early. Her 1993 success was set in amber though it's hardly evergreen. Tom Hanks too, in a sense, has no choice. A Holderlin strategy is not an option for him. Sure, he might legitimately remain proud of his early success. But for the press and his fans, a single season in the career of a top actor does not a life make. Hanks is still considered to be in some kind of ongoing game, in which any success can continue to remain evergreen but is far from set in amber.

Within bounds, though, most of us can choose whether to pursue or eschew the Holderlin strategy. Like a boxer, we can opt to play just a single season and retire as champ, but then watch as that moment of glory recedes into the past. Or we can stay in the ring to accumulate more knockouts—but then risk getting knocked out ourselves and losing the title. Either our accomplishments are secure, set in amber, but then they slip back in time, as with the Holderlin strategy—or else they remain currently relevant, evergreen, but also perpetually insecure, as with the lifelong game.

That is why, for those who pursue the one strategy, the other will always beckon.

Suppose, for example, that you adopted the Holderlin strategy. While still relatively young you won the U.S. Open in golf, and then decided to retire on a high note. No one can take that away from you. You gained hard-won laurels to rest on for the remainder of your life. But then you saw those laurels gradually dissolve into the past. You began to sense people thinking, "That was great, but what has he done lately?" What to do? You don't want to risk getting back in the game.

But that doesn't mean that your game itself—the U.S. Open you won twenty years ago—can't get back in the game. Maybe this year's U.S. Open champ won his match by three strokes. But that's nothing compared to yours, which you won twenty years ago by seven. Or maybe you won yours after the worst drizzle that ever softened a U.S. Open course. Then your championship game is itself still winning new games, triumphing over other championship games. After all, you've found a new ongoing contest in which it continues to reign supreme—still undefeated in the category of best score under postrainy conditions—even though you yourself have long since retired.

Or think of a retired U.S. president (and in terms of strict protocol, he should no longer carry the title of "Mr. President," even though that's how we typically refer to him).[12] Although satisfied with his place in the history books, with his championship season, he will have to watch it fade further and further into the past. And so he will begin to compare his presidency with that of his successors in a variety of novel games of his own devising, sending his presidential term out into new matches against theirs. Consider Bill Clinton, thirteen years after leaving office, favorably stacking his record on income inequality up against that of subsequent presidents.[13] He aspires to set his presidency in amber, while at the same time keeping it evergreen—always entering new competitions, in which he continues to remain the reigning champion. Those who have adopted the Holderlin strategy, trying to shore up for themselves an early engraved-on-the-books victory—Bill Clinton was the third-youngest president—may find themselves restless, prospectively sending that victory out to accumulate fresh conquests in novel games with others.

But the reverse syndrome is also evident: those who have rejected the Holderlin strategy, refusing to fade into history but instead struggling to rack up more and more points over time, may find themselves, toward the end, heading toward a life of overall loss. What to do? Perhaps they can reformulate or reframe one of the victories they scored earlier on, retrospectively elevating it to a single golden "championship season."

"Heh, heh," the reggae star Shaggy chuckled in a 2001 interview with the *Guardian;* "Not bad at all. . . . I [may be only] the second biggest Jamaican artist [after Bob Marley, but] I've sold more records than Bob Marley did in the same space of time." Shaggy was thinking of late 2000, when he had a hit album.[14] He thus turned a losing strategy for a cumulative life-as-a-whole competition into a peak championship in a particular season, which he now attempts to preserve in amber as a special Holderlin moment, years ago.

Donnie Evil, a musician hailing from Bozeman, Montana, is proud of having sold ten records, more than Kanye West did, at Bozeman's Cactus Records in the week before Christmas 2010. "My life's goal was to outsell Kanye at something," Evil told the *Bozeman Daily Chronicle.* "Now I can die happy." Kanye may have walloped

Donnie in cumulative lifetime sales. But Donnie, sifting through his life, found his Holderlin moment.[15]

Neither is pure—the strategy that favors the early triumph nor the one that favors the long haul. Each tugs you toward the other.

A Strange Relationship Between Happiness and Death

Death can never harm us, Epicurus said. As long as we are here, death cannot be. And so it's powerless to interfere with our enjoyment of the goods and pleasures of life. Then as soon as death does arrive, we will have already fled: no longer around to suffer whatever harm or evils it might entail. Throughout the entire process, there will never be a moment when death touches us.

Sound vaguely familiar? This idea bears the same structure as another famous dictum. Known in the ancient world, it is now indelibly associated with Schopenhauer. We can never be happy, Schopenhauer said. As long as we have yet to possess the object of our desire—that boy or girl or beachfront property of our dreams—we will continue to feel the pain and anxiety of unrequited yearning and longing. We'll be driven to distraction by lust or envy and by worries that our quest might fail. And yet as soon as we finally do get our hands on that object, we will discover that our desire for it has fled. The minute we possess it, it will begin losing its capacity to fulfill us, to bring us joy. Almost immediately it will start to bore us or satiate us. We will find fault with it and feel restless. Any fulfillment we reap will be ephemeral, fleeting. Throughout the entire process, there will never be a single moment when complete happiness descends on us.

For Epicurus, when the self is here death isn't; and when death is here the self isn't. For Schopenhauer, when our desire is present the object isn't, and when the object is here our desire isn't. Which raises a question: Does our relationship with death, as Epicurus relates it, in some way mimic our relationship with happiness, as Schopenhauer sees it?

Long before Schopenhauer, the Stoics had already discovered two passageways out of his vicious circle. First, even as you chase after the object of your desire—even while it still remains infuriatingly beyond your grasp—you could keep reminding yourself that if you do succeed in attaining it, any enjoyment you experience will be ephemeral, evanescent, fleeting. That will cool your jets, relieving some of the yearning and longing you feel even as your desire remains yet to be fulfilled. Second, you could, after you do attain the object of your desire, take measures to keep alive the yearning, aspiration, and ambition—the avid longing—that you felt prior to getting it. Doing so will keep you hot for it even while you have it, making your enjoyment of it more lasting than fleeting. You want to continue desiring your wife? Keep imagining her, the Stoics advised, in the arms of someone else.[16]

What we seek, in seeking happiness, are those "gorgeous moments" when "the fulfilled future and the wistful past"—the cool disinterestedness we feel once we attain the object and the hot desire we felt when we were chasing it—"mingle." So said F. Scott Fitzgerald. And he would know.[17]

Suppose, then, that you do manage to bring some of the cooled-off feeling that comes with actually possessing an object into your mind as you are still desirously chasing it. And suppose too that you're able to import some of the hot feelings you felt when you were desirously chasing it into your mind once you have it. Then, the Stoics advised, you can slow down or maybe even stop Schopenhauer's treadmill. Possibly you can even attain those gorgeous moments of which Scott Fitzgerald spoke. And you will thereby find the Holderlin strategy easier to pursue. Once you have had your summer in the sun, you will feel less moved to pursue new desires. You'll foresee how short-lived will be the enjoyment that results from fulfilling them. And you will remain happy with what you have, with that one glorious summer, because you'll take measures to keep alive the pangs of desire you felt for it when it was but a dream lying in the future.

I can't say whether this Stoic strategy for happiness will work for you. It's obviously an individual thing. What I do want to suggest, and it's only a speculative suggestion, is this: to the extent that the Stoic recipe for happiness does work for you, then the Epicurean consolation for death is less likely to.

For many of us, Epicurus's break between our selves and our death—as long as we are here death isn't, and then as soon as death is here we are not—remains too clean and sharp. Our self and its death do meet, at least in a couple of ways.

First, and most obviously, we cannot help but bring a sense of the poignant ephemerality that death portends for us into our mental state well before we die. Though we remain very much alive, we are all too painfully aware of the personal evanescence that our death signifies. And so death is hauntingly present, in our minds if not as an actual fact in the world, even while our selves are still here.

Second, our self's longings and yearnings inevitably extend to facts that will occur in the world well after we die. Will our longing that our grandchild marry her lover and have kids be realized? Will our yearning that Venice not sink into the sea, and the decades of effort we expended on that project, bear fruit? Death makes it impossible for us any longer to enjoy, or ensure the realization of, our self's dearest hopes and wishes.

Epicurus is refuted then: psychologically if not logically. As long as we bring a sense of ephemerality—the ephemerality that death inevitably delivers—into our minds even before we die, and extend our longings to events that will occur in the period after we die, death and our selves will, painfully, overlap. But likewise so is Schopenhauer refuted. As long as we bring a sense of ephemerality—the ephemerality of fulfillment that a desired object will inevitably deliver—into our minds even before we attain it, and extend our longing for that object into the period after we attain it, then we can be happy. So advised the Stoics.

To the extent that we develop a keen and ever-present sense of evanescence and ephemerality, and robust and durable yearnings and longings, we will lament death. But we will also find some measure of (Stoic) happiness. Maybe our capacity for happiness and our sadness about death are connected at some deep level. Or at least the kind of happiness that Holderlin strategists seek after summer's gone.[18]

That Championship Season

Now let's say you've got off on the right track for a Holderlin strategy. You've scored a big triumph early on, and you can then rest on your laurels. Or put it another way: in terms of Epicurus's second consolation your life is now over, in the sense that the narrative arc of your accomplishments has been inscribed safely on the books. It's incapable henceforth of being interrupted or effaced by your demise. Once death comes not only will you, your self, have already left the building, as Epicurus says. Your life, too, in the most crucial sense will have long since been wrapped up. Death won't be able to touch it, to play havoc with it. That's the great advantage of the Holderlin strategy.

But remember: the Holderlin strategy also comes with a disadvantage—one that threatens to creep into your posttriumph period. You might have won the Masters this year. But this year will become last year, then the year before last, then . . . won't you eventually begin to ask yourself, "Great, but what did I do for me lately?" Doesn't that championship season, or summer of the gods, or moment when we were kings, necessarily begin to recede back in time to the point where, after we've been dining out on it for a few years, it would no longer sustain us as it vanishes over the horizon into the past?

No, maybe not necessarily. Think again of the difference between a self and a life. Think of the image of your self—of you—as a jogger, running along the course of your life, whose extension in time is represented by a race track that stretches out in space. The first ten miles correspond to your childhood, the next ten to your adolescence, and so on.

J. David Velleman, whom I discussed in the previous chapter, imagines what it would mean if, instead of running along the course of your life, your self was also stretched out in time right alongside it. If you could see things that way, Velleman argues, then you would avoid the feeling that you were steadily jogging toward your death. Instead, each part of your self would simply focus on whatever part of your life coincided with it, and death would remain completely out of the picture. If you adopted his strategy, Velleman says, then you could more fully avail yourself of Epicurus's first consolation: as long as your self is here, death can't be. It would be wholly irrelevant.

Now think of the Holderlin strategy—the strategy of getting your accomplishments done early and thus gaining psychic access to Epicurus's second consolation: once death comes, nothing of you will be around to be harmed by it. Begin again with the image of yourself running the course of your life. But this time, imagine each mile in the race course of your life, as you run through it, getting up and beginning to trot right alongside of your self. That high-school championship season doesn't remain behind. It jogs abreast of you in lockstep. It endures just as you do.

On this image, that graven-on-the-record period of your life becomes invulnerable not just to your death but even to the passage of time. Your completed and hermetically sealed moment of glory keeps you company apace, and your self can happily trundle on with it close as ever. That championship season needn't recede into the past after all. Not only is it set in amber—no one can dispute the record—but it's also evergreen, so that you need not ask yourself, "What have I done for me lately?" It's as fulfilling to you now as it was when it happened. You will feel no gnawing impetus to seek more triumphs, getting back into the arena where death waits to foil you and interrupt your plans. Your over-and-done life will continue to live on with you. You can then gain the fullest possible psychological access to Epicurus's second consolation: once death comes, both you and your life will lie beyond its clutches.

Is this possible—and if so, how?

In one of the more profound moments on *The Simpsons*, a successful pushcart vendor named Frank recalls how he had once mistakenly believed that he was unsuited for the business of street hawking. That was "the old me," Frank says, "which was, ironically, the young me." It's a deep remark. Why do we refer to the time of Socrates and Aristotle as the Age of Antiquity, when in fact civilization was in its infancy then? Why, as Francis Bacon asked, don't we instead think of our own contemporary time as "the true antiquity . . . inasmuch as it is a more advanced age of the world, and stored and stocked with infinite experiments and observations?"[19]

Perhaps the answer is this: Suppose that we analogize the past 2,500 years of human history to a race course, and humanity itself to an athlete running it. Then certainly humanity—the athlete—is much older now than it was when it was traversing the early parts of the course, such as the time of Socrates and Aristotle. In those days, the Golden Age of Greece, humanity was much younger.

But now suppose that we think of that early part of the race course itself—the time of Socrates and Aristotle, with all its literary and cultural riches—as having got up as humanity ran through it. Dusting itself off, that golden-age-of-Greece era began jogging right alongside humanity, accompanying it into the future instead of disappearing into the past behind it. By now, 2,500 years later, that time will seem ancient. Hence we call it "antiquity," even though humanity itself was much younger when it happened.

At some level, then, it does make sense to say that a past period of time, whether the Golden Age of Athens or, perhaps, our own championship season, can itself endure, can continue to exist—in our minds, of course—as time passes. It can continue to live, and hence grow older, indeed ancient, just as we do. It needn't immediately recede into the past, dead and gone. But when does it make sense to look at moments in time this way—as living and growing old with us instead of dead and gone? What kind of thinking is involved?

An object in space—the Parthenon, say, or the high-school basketball court—doesn't disappear once it's completed. Rather, with each passing year and for as long as it exists, it grows older; it has been with us all the longer. If a given moment in time can somehow be analogized to an object in space, then it too—the Golden Age of Athens, say, or our own championship season—needn't disappear once it's completed either. Instead, that moment itself can stay with us all the way along, growing older with each passing year. Coach, in Jason Miller's *Championship Season*, seems to have made precisely this kind of equation between a moment and an object. He treats the state championship game twenty years earlier not as an event that has long since receded into the past, but—like the trophy that still sits on his shelf—as an object that has accompanied him, very much present and growing old with him, over the years.[20]

Often, though, we mean something very different when we describe events, as opposed to objects, as old. Think, for example, of an event like Damon Runyon's "oldest permanent floating crap game in New York." This kind of event grows old by continuing on indefinitely in time, by never coming to a completion. It doesn't come to an end as did the Golden Age of Greece or the championship game and then—instead of receding back in time—somehow begin growing older along with us the way an object does.

Other kinds of events, while they do come to an end, then become old precisely because they slip back in time, not because they continue living and aging along with us. Think, for example, of the "old" world record in the 100 meters: the record race (9.79 seconds) that Maurice Greene ran in 1999. This usage of "old" does not imply that the record is still with us, that it's gotten older year by year, and that we call it old because of its age as we do an antique object. Instead "old" here implies just the opposite—that something "new" has ended it, that the "old" record has receded in time and is no longer with us. A new record (Usain Bolt, 9.58 seconds) has supplanted the old and left it in the past. It became old precisely because the new terminated it.

So what we're looking for are events that are "old" not because they've never come to a completion like Damon Runyon's "oldest" permanent floating crap game, or because they've slipped back in time like Maurice Greene's "old" running record. On the contrary: we're looking for events that we would call "old" because they have come to a completion and yet stay with us over time—like an object. Like a trophy or a stadium. It's those kinds of events that make possible a Holderlin-style life—one that's over and done but that's still sufficiently present to us that we feel no itch to keep doing more, thereby giving death something to frustrate. But what kinds of events qualify?

Alas. Let's look a little more closely at the kinds of events that we deem to have grown "old" because, after coming to an end, they then aged along with us, like objects. Most in fact are more like units of time than events proper: the good old *days*, olden *times*, the *age* of antiquity. While they did come to an end they were never—as events always can be—terminated. Units of time can't be terminated. They're already terms, the basic terms, of time. Tuesday wasn't terminated by Wednesday, nor was 2013 terminated by 2014—nor was the presidential term of George Bush terminated by the presidential term of Barack Obama—in the way that, say, an old running record gets terminated by a new one. So when we identify a past moment as an "age," or as "times" or "days," we are no longer treating it as an event but rather elevating it out of that realm altogether and conceiving of it as a kind of unit, a basic building block, of time: something that comes to an end but without something else—as can always happen with an ordinary event—putting an end to it. Depending on its meaning to us—whether cultural as with the age of antiquity or sentimental as with "old times"—it can then grow old along with us like a cherished object.[21]

But a specific event like "that championship season"? The men of *That Championship Season*—this is their tragedy—can't seem to see their golden moment the way Coach does. They can't seem to see it as an event that, having ended, then ages along with them like an object, a trophy: something that they can pick up and cradle twenty years later every bit as much as on the day it was won. For some of the men that championship game did end, but then—having been terminated by the final buzzer—it immediately began moving further and further back in time like an old running record. You "can't sit around fingering the past" as if the past were an object, one teammate says.[22] For others, it's as if that championship season is still going on;

they're still delusively living it. It's gotten older simply by never having ended, just like the oldest permanent floating crap game in New York. None of the men can seem to see that championship season as over, ended, *and yet* companionably growing older with them.

Except, of course, for Coach. He alone seems to be able to keep that moment, that event, set in amber and yet still evergreen. He follows Seneca's advice: he treats it as an object, an "everlasting and unanxious possession."

But in fact his tale is the most cautionary.

Social psychologists tell us that the events, or experiences, in our lives—trips, concerts, a great meal—actually make us happier than the objects: cars, necklaces, a snazzy coat. True, experiences vanish in time as soon as they happen. But we often get a warm glow whenever we think of the people with whom we shared them. Objects, by contrast, might last over time. But they tend to be sources of invidious status. We value them, often, precisely because we don't share them with others; we prize them because they distinguish us—they separate us—from our peers. Also, events or experiences, such as the vacation at Yosemite we took last year, tend to be unique. They're less easily compared with alternative events, such as the holiday in Yellowstone we didn't take instead. After all, that trip to Yellowstone never came into existence to begin with, and so no real pound-for-pound comparison is possible. But we can always compare the object we chose—the toaster we bought—to the one we didn't, and feel regret.[23] Because they are both less communal and more comparative, objects generally fail to make us as happy as experiences do.

But the distinction between objects and experiences is not a clean one. Psychologists note that many objects—a flat-screen television, for example—can also be the source of great experiences or events shared with others.[24] And, as with Coach, the arrow would also seem to go the other way. Sometimes great experiences, great events in our lives, become like treasured objects to us. They tend to be precisely those events or experiences, such as championship seasons, that most resemble objects. They are invidious triumphs over competitors. And they do have comparators, such as the scores achieved by others.

Unfortunately, as eventually happens with most of the objects in our life, we inevitably grow tired of and disappointed in such events—and in a way we don't when we treat them as the experiences they are and simply allow them to slip back in time once they've happened. Coach encounters precisely this kind of fatigue and disillusionment at the end of the play. The event that he has treated as an object to cherish and coddle—that championship game—finally, after the coup de grâce of a disillusioning evening with his now-middle-aged team, becomes, like any object eventually will, cold and dull. In fact it crumbles. It utterly loses its capacity, as psychologists tell us many an object ultimately will, to make him happy. Far better that he had treated it as an event, an experience, and—allowing it to begin sliding back in time the moment it was done—then struck out for new ones. He might have felt wistful about it. But he wouldn't have mourned it, as he does when that championship season finally dies to him.

Events are not supposed to persist in time the way objects like trophies do. Instead, once over, they are meant to disappear backward in time beyond our grasp. Not only is that how most of us unavoidably do look at the moments of our lives, it's how (and here Coach is a cautionary tale) we ought to look at them. But in that case, Epicurus's second consolation—that once death comes there will be nothing of ourselves that it can harm—will finally have little psychological resonance with us. We can try to get our life over and done with so that death can't harm it, as the Holderlin strategy recommends. But then we must watch it recede ever further into the past. And so we risk becoming the chief mourners of our own life.[25]

three

LOOK WHO'S CALLING HIMSELF NOTHING

An old joke: A rabbi enters the synagogue sanctuary and, looking around to make sure no one else is present, gets down on his knees, beats his breast, and cries "O Lord, what am I compared to thee? I am nothing. Nothing!" He rises and is about to leave by a side door when in comes the cantor, who, not seeing the rabbi, also falls to his knees, gazes heavenward, and moans, "Lord, compared to thy greatness I am nothing! Nothing, do you hear me? Nothing!" Getting up and brushing himself off, the cantor moves to the side door where he sees the rabbi; the two exchange pleasantries and are about to leave when in comes the beadle—the synagogue caretaker. Furtively glancing around and, not seeing the rabbi and the cantor, he too kneels, throws back his head, and wails, "In thine eyes my Lord, what am I? I am nothing! Nothing, I tell you! Nothing!" At which point the cantor turns to the rabbi, elbows him playfully in the ribs, and scoffs, "Look who's calling himself 'nothing.'"

I think of this joke when I reflect on the Buddhist consolation for death. To spend our life tenaciously pursuing a set of self-focused projects and attachments, Buddhist wisdom argues, is to court suffering whenever they end in disappointment. And they inevitably will. Far better to abandon any concern with our self. Indeed, far better to recognize, with the help of various Buddhist insights, that there is no such thing as the self to begin with. It's a mere mental construct, a figment of our mind. It is, in fact, nothing. We need not suffer from worldly pain and loss because *we*—our selves—do not exist. There is no subject that undergoes any such pain and loss, no subject to whom that suffering belongs. The trick is simply to see this.[1]

There's an added bonus: Since our self is the very thing that we are supposed to lose when we die, death—once we understand that the self doesn't exist to begin with—will then become a nonevent for us, not worth fretting over. This is the Buddhist consolation. Its central idea of self-abandonment—not Buddhism as a whole in all its richness—is my topic here.

It's not true, as some critics of Buddhism argue, that by abandoning our sense of self we cease to have any reason to live. Even if our self—along with our ego, our selfishness, our anxieties for our own success—disappear, our life—its sensuality, its compassion for others, the joy we feel when we use it to repair the world—continues. "Have I ever hated life?" Thomas Buddenbrook asks—"pure, relentless life? Folly and misconception! I have but hated myself, because I could not bear it. But I love [life]."[2]

There's a contrast to be made between the Buddhist consolation and Epicurus's first consolation, at least as ways of life. By barring all thoughts of death from our minds as we do when we follow Epicurus's first consolation—as long as we are here, death cannot be and so remains irrelevant—we risk failing to wrap our life up. As a result, while our self ends at death, much of our life, with its uncompleted projects and unresolved relationships, continues on without it. On the Buddhist consolation, however, our self ends long before we die. It ends at the moment we realize it doesn't exist, while our life, with its sensuousness and richness, continues on without it.

Buddhism, of course, is a religion. Many of its tenets rely on spiritual or mythological claims that go beyond this world and so, too, beyond the premises of my discussion here. I will, consequently, look at the Buddhist consolation ultimately through the lenses of Western philosophers such as Oxford's Derek Parfit and Princeton's Mark Johnston, who have adapted its teachings for a nonbelieving audience, and who, personally, find them consoling. I focus, then, on the simple core of the Buddhist consolation—no self, no death—and I look at it in a freestanding way, detached from its central role as part of the Buddhist progression from samsara to nirvana.

The "self is nothing," one Buddhist scholar writes.[3] The "self is nothing but an illusion," the self is nothing more than a "conditional semiotic construct," "there is no self per se at all," say others.[4] The "self does not exist"; "the self is nothing."[5] I am uneasy about this.

I imagine Death, relaxing in an armchair, thumbing through recent writings on Buddhist views of the self. Shaking his head, Death chuckles quietly: "Heh, heh, heh . . . look who's being called nothing."

But perhaps this is unfair to the Buddhist consolation. The other "death is benign" consolations, too, try to defang nothingness. Either they deny the horror of the nothingness that awaits after death or they celebrate the beauty of the various nothingnesses to be found during life. Each does so in its own way.

In Epicurus's first consolation—as long as we are here, death can't be—"nothingness" comes off as utterly harmless. By definition, death's "nothingness" can't ever be experienced. There's no such thing as a subject of nothingness. After all, if there is anything—anything at all, even a bare subject—then there isn't nothing. Nothingness, then, is self-neutralizing and so completely benign.

In Epicurus's second consolation—once death comes, we are no longer here to be harmed by it—"nothingness" is actually a consummation devoutly to be wish'd. The best thing we can do is try to get all our accomplishments, the Sturm und Drang of life, behind us as soon as possible. We would then abide for the remainder of our days in utter calm and imperturbability. After all, we'd have nothing to lose to death, simply because there would be nothing anymore to our lives. And once we understood that this attractive state of nothingness in life doesn't really differ all that much from the nothingness of death, we'd easily glide from one nothingness into the other.

Finally in existentialism, nothingness—just like death—is necessary for the very existence of our self. "Nothing," of course, is the opposite of "everything." And so Sartre applies the term "nothingness" to our human capacity to negate reality, to transcend everything that actually exists and think about what doesn't. Without the possibility of nothingness, we couldn't follow our own authentic choices. Instead they'd be dictated by the existing reality around us.[6]

Each consolation, in its own way, thus slyly domesticates nothingness, making it serve the purposes of its own key idea.

According to the Buddhist consolation, the self—the ostensible victim of death's nothingness—doesn't exist. It's nothing itself: a mental illusion.

According to Epicurus's first consolation, a subject—an ostensible victim—of death's nothingness can't exist. It's nothing itself: a metaphysical impossibility.

According to Epicurus's second consolation, nothingness is a good thing. It's synonymous with imperturbability and calm.

According to the existentialist consolation, nothingness is a good thing. It's synonymous with imagination and creativity.

The four consolations, without ever intending it—they certainly weren't consulting each other on the matter—have each tried to take nothingness back from death. Buddhism is not alone in this regard. Put another way: death might find something to chuckle about in each of the four consolations.[7]

Breath and Shadow

Since I—and possibly you—will never know what the Buddhist experience of self-less-ness (or no-self) is like, it's worth considering the metaphors that Buddhist saints and scholars use to convey it to the noninitiate. Those metaphors originate in the need to depict life in the absence of all of the motives, cognitive structures, and passions that make up the self. No motives or cognitive categories or passions, in other words, no self. No self, no selfish desire. No selfish desire, no suffering—because suffering comes from the frustration of desire. And of course no self, no death. So here, I look at what it means to abandon the self, to abandon all our motives, cognitive categories, and passions, while still remaining alive.

Consider first what it could mean to live without the motives that are so definitive of a self.[8] Denuding ourselves of all motives, all motivation, would allow us to cultivate an indifference to whatever happens, thus deflating desire. Critics of Buddhism retort that by becoming demotivated we would simply render life passive and inert. Buddhist scholars, as I read them, reply that there's a world of difference between motivation and animation. We can still be animated by the energy of life without being motivated by our own selfish schemes and desires. To convey what this means— to show how we can banish selfish motivation and yet still remain animated—Buddhist writings metaphorically cast a selfless life as a kind of "breath," "wind," or "spirit."[9]

Breath, wind, and spirit certainly resonate with the idea of pure animation—they move—but without motivation: they are empty. Yet they are revealing metaphors because at their core they gesture to a kind of equivocation, a borderland or netherworld. A breath, wind, or spirit is neither air nor liquid but something hovering in between: air—empty, devoid of animus—but air that flows like a liquid, that's animated. A spirit too, in ancient Greek and Hebrew, is a fluid vapor.[10]

Now hold that thought, and consider next what it means to banish the cognitive categories that so structure the self. How would doing so diminish our desires, and hence our suffering? Suppose that we came to understand that the objects that we chase after, the objects that we think would fulfill our desires—wealth, status, material things, beautiful men or women—do not really exist. They, and hence the very idea of desire-fulfillment, are but chimerical concepts that we impose on the raw flow of experience. All that such cognitive categories ultimately do is lure us into the false belief that the desiderata they conjure up are actual realities—and hence encourage us only to desire and cling to them.[11]

We can explode these illusions, these figments, if we learn to engage the world directly in their absence. What would that feel like? Buddhist writers have offered provocative images for what remains when life's experiences flow unstructured by the desiring self's cognitive categories. The raw flow of experience resembles "salt in brine," "oil in sesame seeds," or "butter in curds."[12] Notably, these and similar images gesture toward something that is neither liquid nor solid, but rather a mixture of the two. And it makes sense that Buddhist thinkers would gravitate to such metaphors. For to grasp the idea of life as a flow of raw experience, we need the viscous imagery of a no-man's-land between liquid—flow—and solid: all the phenomena that make up the people and objects of experience, but that swirl into each other when there are no conceptual borders separating them.

Finally, consider what it would mean to rid ourselves of the roiling passions that so deeply constitute the self. You can sap the power of desire, Buddhist wisdom says, by learning to perceive or "notice" the events of your life dispassionately, as if from a distance. View your own life, in other words, as if you were an external spectator to it. In that way, you will develop no self-interested passionate or emotional response to what you perceive—although you could still feel the same third-party *com*passion concerning your life's events as you would for any other life's. As far as you are concerned, then, your life would simply be a series of perceptions—or awarenesses—devoid of affective significance for you.[13] The Dalai Lama once illustrated this principle in his usual gently captivating way. Occasionally, when he sees a woman who tempts him, His Holiness quickly calls himself up short, reminding himself "I am monk!" and emotionally distancing himself from that "image of the eye."[14]

What metaphors do Buddhist writers use to convey a sense of such a life—one that we would simply perceive as "images of the eye" without reacting to its events in a selfishly passionate way? They describe such a life as an ongoing interplay of reflections and shadows. Or light and shade.[15] Those seem like reasonable images to convey the idea of pure perceptions, devoid of the capacity to provoke emotional response. But what, in turn, are reflections and shadows? They're simply entities that flirt with the boundary between solid and air—different kinds of solids that are no more substantial than air.

One cannot, ultimately, be told directly and literally what a selfless life would be like. If we seek to know it truly and non-metaphorically, only years of practice will suffice. Even so, Buddhist metaphors for depicting to the noninitiate what remains when the self dissolves—for depicting life without a self, or a selfless life—are keenly revealing.

What they disclose is a struggle to get across the idea of a life that's animated but not motivated, experienced but not in a cognitive way, and perceived but not in a passionate manner. That's what life shorn of the self would be like. But crucially, the struggle to get it across to the noninitiate has come to center on a kind of symbolism that's almost not of this world—that exists at the interstices of air, liquid, and solid: not any of them, but somehow betwixt and between. A selfless life is a kind of liquid air—breath, wind, spirit, and moving vapor—or a solidish liquid—runny butter, viscous sesame oil, water clouded with particulate salt—or an airy solid: shadow, light, reflection, and shade. Neither air nor liquid nor solid. If the self truly doesn't exist, does it not seem as if life barely would either?[16]

Self-Effacement

Celebrities often refer to themselves in the first-person plural, as "we." "For two years," Garth Brooks said in an interview with the *Independent* in 2007, "we couldn't find anything that we wanted to be an actor in."[17] Other famous people speak of themselves not in the first-person plural but in the third-person singular: "I've been very careful that Deborah Norville does the right thing," the TV personality Deborah Norville once told the *Seattle Times;* "Deborah has been pretty clever about managing her associations."[18]

These rhetorical tics are far from uncommon. Martha Stewart shows a partiality for using the first-person plural, "we," to refer to herself. Regis Philbin opts for the third-person singular, "he." And the actor Richard Dreyfuss uses both.[19] Perhaps, one day, he will simply start referring to himself as "they."

Viewed one way, these two modes of referring to oneself seem aligned with Buddhist notions of self-abandonment or self-effacement. Each allows a person to refer to himself without, actually, referring to his self.

And indeed some Buddhist thinkers do explicitly advocate dissolving the self—the "I"—into the first-person plural, into the "we." An individual should identify his aims and projects with those of mankind as a whole, the Buddhist writer David Loy says. Once a person recognizes that there is no "I" but only the ongoing flow of human life, Loy claims, the "I" will become "us." Other Buddhist writers, arguing for a detached view of the self, in effect recommend that we each view ourselves in the third-person singular, as a removed "he" or "she." Observing our self from a distance, as if it were somebody else, we will become emancipated from the suffering it undergoes.

When pressed, celebrities who refer to themselves in these two no-self ways, as either "we" or "s/he" instead of "I," do give a more or less Buddhist account of their usage. The singer Neal McCoy is fond of referring to himself in the first-personal plural, as "we." In doing so he claims to be acknowledging, in a self-deprecating way, that his success results from a team effort requiring an entourage of managers, agents, writers, and directors.[20] There is no "I" involved in McCoy's projects and plans, no ego or self, only "we."

Meanwhile the baseball player Wade Boggs, in using the third-person singular "he" to denote himself, says that he does so lest it seem that, by referring to himself as "I," he would be boasting. Whoever it is that has achieved baseball glory, Boggs is saying, it is not I. Instead, Boggs self-effacingly places himself at a remove from the "he" who has those feats to his credit.[21] The elder George Bush went halfway in this direction, not referring to himself as "he" but dropping the "I" so as to distance himself modestly from whomever it was who scored all his accomplishments.

Both McCoy and Boggs claim to be jettisoning the self in more or less Buddhist fashion. But that's not how we hear it. After all, we have come to think of the use of "we" and "he" to refer to oneself as just the opposite of Buddhist-style self-effacement: such coinages are about as self-aggrandizing as you can get. They are poster children of unrestrained ego. Referring to yourself as "we" suggests not that you have submerged yourself in the onrush of humanity but that—as with the "royal we"—you have submerged humanity in your grandiose self, that you view yourself and your needs as equal ing concern will be the same as ours: to have their name on the lips of their successors. . . . How does that confer any reality on us?" Far from being our collaborators in the project of keeping our memory alive, our children will turn into our competitors. I remember once wandering into a religious center in North Toronto and peering at the plaques on the classroom doors. Many took this form (names have been changed):

THIS ROOM HAS BEEN DEDICATED BY
EARL AND SONIA JOHNSON
in loving memory of
their mother Leah Johnson

In our era, if not long before, "death denial" has expanded to include "death-of-memory denial." Most academic sociologists expect to still be remembered, by colleagues in the field, fifty years from now.[12]

Shelley's poem "Ozymandias" conjures up the image of an ancient, decapitated, and trunkless statue in the desert. The decaying pedestal reads, "My name is Ozymandias, King of Kings: Look on my works, ye mighty, and despair!" And yet no works, no marks, nothing but the "lone and level sands" remain, stretching endlessly in all directions.

Imagine, though, that the marks Ozymandias made long ago had not crumbled into sand but had somehow remained with us, weathered but majestic in their desert space. Say that they took the form of a great city of marble, alabaster, and pink granite.[13] Yes, visiting tourists would be able to answer the question "Who built this city?" It was Ozymandias. And yes, they could answer the question "Who was Ozymandias?" He was the builder of the city. But in knowing the name and the marks—which simply refer back to each other in an endless arid loop—would they have come any closer to remembering the man, the person, than if they had never heard of him or his marks?

Suppose we are tourists beholding Ozymandias's works, clutching our water bottles and snapping pictures with our phones. But now suppose, if I can adapt an old philosophical joke, that our tour guide rushes up to us with some late-breaking news. It's just been discovered that all of these marks—the city's buildings in all their splendor—weren't built by Ozymandias after all. Instead, they were built by some other guy who also happened to be named Ozymandias. That would have no meaning for us. Nothing in our sense of Ozymandias would change because there is nothing to our sense of Ozymandias. The same name, the same marks—they could, for all we can bring to mind, have belonged to anybody.

By contrast, a similar discovery about Churchill—Winston Churchill did not deliver the "We Shall Never Surrender" speech; it was in fact orated by some other man named Winston Churchill—would carry the shock of a thunderbolt. That's because while Ozymandias's name and marks don't make us recall a particular person, Churchill's do: even though we never met either one.

For someone to place his imprint on the minds of future generations on into time—for someone to remain alive in memory—simply engraving his name and his marks in various spaces, physical and cyber, won't suffice, even if those marks are great in number. Those gazing at them must have spent time with them. But how much time? Whatever time it takes for them to no longer feel that the marks could have been made by anyone—by any other person who happened to have been named Ozymandias—because those marks have solidified and jelled into one particular person in their mind.

This is, of course, a psychological and not a logical process. The person we have in mind when we think of Churchill might turn out to bear only a partial resemblance to the real Churchill. But then we invariably get our recollections of people terribly wrong all the time, profoundly misunderstanding them even if we actually have met them, even if we actually have spent time with them. Couple that with the likelihood that few of those who actually did meet Churchill in person spent nearly as much time in his actual presence as others, like his biographer Martin Gilbert, have spent thinking about, pondering, and steeping themselves in Churchill's marks, his words or actions, even though they never encountered him. There's no reason to think that our memory of a person we have met is necessarily more accurate than those of others who may have never met him. Especially if they have spent much more time with his marks than we ever spent with him, the person.

Saul Kripke devised his theory of reference in opposition to a rival theory (or set of theories) called descriptivism. Descriptivism, to simplify dramatically, says that a name attaches to a particular set of marks, even if in principle the person who made those marks could have been anyone. According to descriptivism, for example, we have come to use the name "Kurt Gödel" to refer to the person who discovered the Incompleteness Theorem. But suppose one day we learn that the person who discovered the Incompleteness Theorem was not in fact the man at Princeton we always thought was the one who accomplished that feat, but a woman at Duke. Then, according to descriptivism, *she* would be the person to whom we were always referring with the name "Kurt Gödel." And, Kripke said, that just doesn't make any sense.

So descriptivism—which says that the name straightforwardly attaches to the marks, even though the person who made them could in theory be anyone—doesn't seem to capture what it is to use a name to refer to someone. Descriptivism, though, does seem to capture a central truth about what it is to remember someone—and, in particular, someone we have never met. All we can ever know is that a name attaches to a given set of marks. Beyond that, as far as we are concerned in the vast majority of cases, that person could have been anyone. Perhaps descriptivism was always a better fit as a theory of remembrance than of reference.

Likewise, what Kripke offered is a better theory of reference than remembrance. Kripke said that a name refers to a particular person, even though that person could have made any set of marks. So yes, when people on into the future speak the name "Nat Bailey" as they encounter it on a plaque, they will indeed be referring to the one particular person Nat Bailey—to him and no other—even if they have never heard of him before. But Nat Bailey would have been mistaken if he thought that those people would be *remembering* him:

that *he* would be living on in their memory. While the name "Nat Bailey" certainly refers to the particular person Nat Bailey, it can't make us remember the person Nat Bailey, call *him* in particular to mind. He could have been anyone. What Kripke offered was simply a theory of reference. It was not—as so many of us implicitly seem to think when we post our name and marks on buildings or benches—a theory of remembrance.[14]

In his great book *Naming and Necessity*, Kripke himself says something quite revealing. While he can imagine Aristotle never actually doing "any of the things"—making any of the marks—"commonly attributed to him today," such as composing the *Ethics* and the *Politics*, he can't imagine Hitler ever having done anything other than evil. But then recognizing that such a statement sits uneasily with his theory that a name attaches to a person regardless of what marks he might have made, Kripke immediately backtracks. Hitler, Kripke acknowledges, "might have spent all his days [quietly] in Linz." And had he done so, Kripke says, he still would have been Adolf Hitler, because "Adolf Hitler" is the name his parents gave to that particular person, not to a particular set of horrific marks left upon the world.[15]

I think what Kripke was saying, with his little slip, was not that the person to whom the name "Hitler" refers couldn't have spent a quiet life in Linz, leaving none of his evil marks on the world. It's that the evil marks in question could have been made by no one else but the person in Kripke's mind, in all of our minds, whom we remember as Hitler. We have spent enough time with the name, and the marks, that the name is no longer just a phrase for whomever it was who made those marks. We know who that person is, even though we never met him. He—not just his name and deeds—will live in infamy.

Remembrance of someone we have never met is based on an ongoing temporal process. It's based on the repeated acts of thinking about, and dwelling on, the marks attached to a name. That makes sense. After all, the self, as we bundles of ego and anxiety think of it, is an entity that needs to move ever forward in time if it's to continue living. And so, once it dies, it can continue to move forward in time—in memory, of course—only if at least some people continue spending enough time with the name and the associated marks that a distinct self emerges and continues to abide in their minds over the years, decades, and centuries. Otherwise, for them, that name and those marks could have belonged to anyone, "whoever she may be."

But for most of us mortals, our selves will not live on through our name and whatever marks we leave for the future, even if others, on into the ages, read them or see them. On into the future, those others will not spend the time necessary for a sense of our self to emerge in their minds and move forward with them. A name and a set of marks recorded on a spatial or cyberspatial object—a plaque or a website—might refer to us. But that won't suffice to enable others to remember us, to make our self live on in their memory. They won't be thinking of anyone in particular. The consolation for mortality that I have identified with Nat Bailey, on which our mere name and marks imprinted on the future can keep our mortal selves alive in a way that intimates immortality, won't work. Not for almost all of us.

*

Can mortality, in any meaningful way, intimate immortality? Can I realize, within the confines of my mortal life, the various good things that immortality seems to promise?

Yes, says Gordon Bell. All I have to do is record the moments of my life, the entire contents of my memory, in real-time audio, video, and textual files and then post them online. Those moments will then remain alive indefinitely as long as others, on into the unending eons, view them in my digitized life-log. And so I myself don't have to live on to keep my cherished memories, my own precious trove of knowledge of the past, alive forever. Anyone else can do that for me.

And yes, mortality might be as good as immortality if I can, in my twilight years, attain "closure." Suppose, as death nears, that I am able to "close the door" or "turn the latch" on the moments of my life, leaving them pristine ever after as if they occupied some kind of sealed room or cell. Then I wouldn't have to live on to fight with others over what my life meant, over the main lines of its narrative, over the significance of its events. My imprint on my own past, the meaning I gave my own life, would be the definitive one.

And yes, mortality might be as good as immortality if it makes sense for me to equate my self with what the philosopher Mark Johnston calls a bare "quasi-spatial arena." Then, even though that arena will disappear with my death, I could still access whatever precious knowledge others might amass—about the secrets of God or consciousness or the universe—on into the future. All I would need to do while alive is place all future humans, instead of Andrew Stark, at the center of my arena, leading a life dedicated to their interests. And then whatever knowledge they accumulated during their lives on into the millennia would belong to me no less than it would belong to those future humans. After all, my claim to their lives would be just as strong as theirs. That's because all there is to making any given life one's own is choosing to place it at the focus of one's arena.

And finally, yes, mortality might be as good as immortality if it makes sense for me to view my self as if it were nothing more than the mere referent of my name. Then, as long as people are reading that name on into the future, whether on a wall plaque or in a book dedication, they will be keeping me—the person I was—alive in memory. I myself don't have to live on for my self to live on. My imprint on the future, the marks I made during my mortal life, will keep me alive. In the minds of others, if not in the world.

Unfortunately none of these ingenious ideas speaks to our central psychological reality. Certainly not for us bundles of ego and anxiety who seek consolation for our mortality. Our self, as we see it, is something that must move relentlessly forward into the future if it is to survive. It's hardly the mere referent of a name. Or a bare arena. For us, too, the moments of our lives must flow back ever further into the past as soon as they happen. They can never be permanently freeze-dried into mere files on a server. Or preserved as pristine items in a locked room. And so they are fated to become forever irrecoverable in the intimate ways in which we ourselves knew them, yet ever vulnerable to the foreign interpretations others on into the future will place on them.

The self as the mere referent of a name. Or a bare arena. The moments of our lives as files on a server. Or items in a locked room. Referents, files, arenas, and rooms are dry, static husks. In order to believe that our mortal selves and our mortal lives could even begin to give us the good things that their immortal versions would, we have to pretend that those selves and lives are bare shadows of what they actually are. We have to pretend that they are already halfway dead.

And so mortality cannot intimate, cannot give us, the good things that immortality would. We shall have to look elsewhere for consolation. Perhaps if we view matters in the right way, we will see that immortality—real immortality, not the intimated sort—would be terrible for us. I turn to this consolatory idea in the book's next part.

PART 3

Immortality Would Be Malignant

IS THIS ALL THERE IS?

It's evening in Lake Como. The young music professor Shawmut, in Saul Bellow's story "Him with His Foot in His Mouth," reads his conference paper to Kippenberg, an older and far more prominent musicologist, author of the definitive work on Rossini and bearer of "eyebrows like caterpillars from the Tree of Knowledge." Worried that his prose is failing to impress the great man, Shawmut sheepishly remarks: "I'm afraid I'm putting you to sleep, Professor." The master replies: "No, no — on the contrary, you're keeping me awake."[1]

As if it were thumbing its nose at its own reputation for monotony and uniformity, boredom has gone out into the world and amassed for itself an impressive variety of classifications and categorizations. Stendhal distinguished between "still" versus "bustling" boredoms.[2] For the philosopher Sean Healy, what's key is the dichotomy between the boredom of "restlessness" and the boredom of "torpor."[3] Heidegger offered discriminations between the limbo boredom of waiting for a train, the empty boredom of attending a cocktail party, and the deeper boredom that comes from personal inauthenticity — from leading a life that isn't your own.

But I like Bellow's distinction the best. The exchange between Shawmut and Kippenberg captures two immediately recognizable strains of boredom. If you are experiencing the one, then however much you would prefer to be in a state of unconsciousness than continue listening to (say) Professor X's tedious lecture on associative learning in sea slugs, you can't nod off because the rattling of his voice and clanking of the air conditioner are keeping you awake. If you are undergoing the other, then however much you might like to listen to Professor Y's informative lecture on consolations for mortality, you can't because his droning delivery and the murmur of the heating system are putting you to sleep.

Now think of the two types of endless boredom that different writers, seeking to console us for our mortality, have predicted would be our sorry fate if we were immortal. Each simply extends one of these dual themes. On the first scenario, the problem with immortality would be that over enough time, we humans would experience everything that a person possibly can experience. But we would no more be able to seek relief in death from the world's now-wearisome noise than you, sitting in Professor X's class, can seek relief in sleep from his continued tedious natterings. Call this the boredom of exquisite ennui. In the other scenario, the problem with immortality is that, almost immediately, a deep inertia would descend upon immortals, preventing them from experiencing anything at all. No matter how worthwhile or tempting any experience might be, immortals would feel no more urgency about seeking it out—knowing that they could always get around to it later—than you would feel about staying awake during Professor Y's informative lecture, if you knew that you could always view it tomorrow online or read his book. Call this the boredom of profound lethargy.[4]

So: for those who believe that immortality would be cosmically boring, there are two scenarios. After enough time has passed, immortals would eventually feel that they have seen absolutely everything, and so suffer profound ennui. Or else right from the outset, they would do absolutely nothing and so suffer profound lethargy. Yet in fact, these seemingly opposite possibilities are simply two sides of the same coin.

Think of a trip to the Eiffel Tower. At the most abstract level, with all the specific details bleached out, one trip is like any other. At the most concrete level, by contrast, with all the details factored in—the precise angle of the sun, the haze in the air, the acidity of the rain the previous night, and the way the Tower accordingly glints and glistens—no one trip is like any other.

Now: The more abstractly we view the events of our life absent any of the differentiating details—the more this year's visit to the Tower, for example, seems just like last year's—the sooner we will conclude that we have seen everything and thus begin to experience the boredom of ennui. But equally, the more abstractly we view the events of our life absent any of the differentiating details—the more we expect that a visit to the Tower next year will be just like one we might take this year, so why rush?—the more likely we also are to do nothing, put things off, and experience the boredom of lethargy.

The two boredoms—the twin boredoms that those who would console us for our mortality foresee in immortality—can thus coexist, because they emerge from the same worldview. It's a view of the world shorn of specificities, understood by immortals in terms of simple abstract universals. And the issue is not simply that one trip to the Eiffel Tower becomes like any other, but that one trip no matter where becomes just like any other trip no matter where. Then one activity becomes like any other. And finally, at an abstract enough level, life itself comes to be a single undifferentiated and unending event, an unwavering gray haze, "the humming of a single sound in the ear," as the poet Anthony Hecht puts it. Or a "gnawingly hypnotic rotary hum so total it might have been silence itself," as David Foster Wallace says.[5] At this abstract level, "all things" become, in the words of Lucretius, "the same forever."[6] Once they have come to look at the world this way, bored immortals will conclude that they have seen everything and find that they have the motivation to do nothing. Ennui and lethargy converge.

In this way our experience of immortality would strangely mirror God's experience of eternity, at least as imagined by medieval church fathers.[7] Since God exists outside of time, all of time is spread out before Him in a single vista. He can see everything that has ever happened and that ever will happen. And yet, theologians have argued, a timeless God would actually do nothing—at least, nothing that resembles human action. After all, actions can take place only in time, and He abides outside of it.[8] Doing nothing, while having seen everything there is to see: not much suspense or excitement in God's experience of eternity. No more, perhaps, than would result from human immortality, in which we too, sooner or later, would do nothing while having seen everything there is to see. As long as God can't do much better with eternity than we could with immortality, maybe—so the boredom consolationists might suggest—mortality isn't so bad after all.

But if immortal life would be boring, then wouldn't it also offer the mechanisms that we mortals have always had available to snap out of boredom, or even turn it to good use? In our mortal existence as it is, the Sanskrit scholar Wendy Doniger notes, boredom introduces times of "temporary death" into life, allowing a person to withdraw —to take an extended time-out if necessary—and then return to the world refreshed.[9] Periods of boredom and world-weariness came to be viewed as wholly bad things only in the twentieth century, Patricia Meyer Spacks argues in her 1995 book *Boredom;* in much of Western thought boredom was welcomed as a kind of "suspended attention" that allows for "semi-conscious brooding" and "makes a space for creativity."[10] Why, then, should immortal boredom not redeem itself in the same way: by instilling, even into immortal life, periods of rejuvenating "temporary" death? We could then enjoy the advantages of both immortality—living forever—and mortality— dying periodically to restock our creative juices—without the evils of each.

But how, exactly, does boredom lead to creativity? How does it snap out of itself? What are the mechanisms? A preferred kind of imagery has emerged to illustrate the answer to this question: boredom is like a prison cell. A "solitary prisoner for life," Kierkegaard says, "is extremely resourceful; to him a spider can be a source of great amusement." You'd think with just a spider to occupy him all day long the inmate would be bored forever, but he will eventually learn to provoke the insect, prod it, play with it, turn it over and over in the changing light, follow its every unpredictable move for hours on end every day, thus sooner or later replacing boredom with creativity and intrigue.[11] Camus' prisoner Merseault, too, "end[s] up not being bored at all." In jail awaiting execution, Merseault observes

I keep thinking about my room and, in my imagination, I'd set off from one corner and walk around making a mental note of everything I saw on the way . . . I'd remember every piece of furniture . . . every object and, on every object, every detail, every mark, crack or chip and then even the colour or the grain of the wood. . . . I realized that a man . . . could easily live for a hundred years in prison. He'd have enough memories not to get bored.[12]

For these inmates, Kierkegaard's and Camus', their cells—which seemingly cut them off from all that's entertaining in the world, thereby threatening interminable boredom—in fact still necessarily contain some "objects," as Merseault says. And objects, however humble—spiders, cracks in the wall, grains in the wood—can, at one point, begin drawing the mind down unplumbably deep wells of fascination.

I am not saying that I necessarily buy any of this. I am saying only that the prisoner in his cell seems to be the default metaphor for those who want to suggest that boredom—emptiness, idleness, a vacuity of experience—can provide space for the mind to wander, noodle around, take its time, and become expansive, creative, and imaginative, so that ultimately boredom expunges itself. Arthur Koestler, too, sees the confined space of the prison cell as the crucible for boredom's chrysalis into stimulation. In *Dialogue with Death* Koestler writes: "Memorable events are understood, in the murky bell-jar of the prison, [to be] things like . . . a spider in the window, a bug in the bed. These are breath-taking experiences; they employ and stimulate the free-running mechanism of thought for hours at a time. They are substitutes for visits to the movies, making love, reading the newspapers . . . "[13] The question, though, is whether these images of confined spatial boredom apply in any way to the boundless temporal boredom that immortality threatens.

They don't. Kierkegaard, Camus, and Koestler mean to suggest that even if our life's confined circumstances reduce us to just one single solitary object, a spider or a table, that object can nevertheless always provoke any number of new mental events—an endless flow of "free-running" thoughts. And so mortal boredom can always be transcended. The problem with immortal boredom, though, would be just the opposite: the world would remain full of any number of objects, from Eiffel Towers to espressos. But all of them would eventually occasion the same single solitary event in our mind: a humming sound so all pervasive that, as David Foster Wallace says in describing the most excruciating boredom he can imagine, it's no different than silence itself. A single sound, a sound that's at the same time a nonsound; a single event that's at the same time a nonevent. As the 342-year-old Elina Makropoulos puts it in Karel Čapek's play *The Makropoulos Secret*, "Singing is the same as keeping silent. Everything is the same. There's no difference in anything."[14] And it's hard to see how, if and when we ever get into such a state, we would then get out of it.

Think of it this way: new "events," as Koestler says, can always happen to the same persisting object, say a spider. We can run it through our fingers, set it in a quest up the wall, imagine it's an alien creature invading our cot. And so we remain engaged. But new events cannot happen to the same continuing event, say a hum.[15] If they do, it's a different event. And so what if we have, as immortals, reached a point where we see all events as the same, as "intolerably identical?"[16] Could we ever break out of it?

I am in no position to say whether boredom would be our lot if we lived forever, and in the following chapters I consider some alternatives. The question here is whether, assuming boredom *is* our immortal fate—assuming that immortality comes to feel like a single event unfolding in limitless time—the mortal-boredom metaphor of a single object placed in limited space would capture it, giving us reason for hope. It wouldn't.

In his memoir *Miracles of Life*, J. G. Ballard writes of the teenage years he spent with his family in Lunghua, a World War II Japanese prison camp. Something different, though, happened at this prison: the boredom of bounded space somehow shifted into the boredom of boundless time. At one point, Ballard recalls, the prisoners ceased to find the various objects around them—chess sets, old magazines, discarded toys—even minimally stimulating. Why? Because all these objects had begun to furnish exactly the same undifferentiated experience or event—or more exactly the same nonevent or nonexperience. The camp had become an "eventless world," Ballard writes, of irreversible, "crushing boredom.[17] And so too would the immortal boredom that death consolationists foresee, should it be our fate, come with no redeeming features, no goad to creativity. No way out. Better, then, that we remain mortal than experience that kind of fate.

Any hopeful scenario for immortal boredom, based on the ways in which mortal boredom can be self-correcting, must confront the fact that events do not persist in time the way objects do. Yes, even a single object in a confined space—think of a child in her bedroom with just a cardboard box to play with—may be able to provoke any number of events over time, and so allow for an escape from boredom. But once the same single event in endless time—the same continuing undifferentiated hum—is provoked by any number of objects, interminable boredom sets in. Immortal boredom would be far worse than the mortal kind. Once it took hold, it would be inescapable. And in this way, the "boredom" consolation for mortality does have validity.

ten

STILL LIFE

A human life, the philosopher Timothy Chappell writes, "is a rope of overlapping threads." At any given time, some threads—some episodes in our life—are coming to an end. Others are in the middle of their duration. And still others are just beginning. As long as this "overlapping" persists, then even if the threads at one end are entirely different from those at the other, it's the same life all the way through. Just as it would be the same rope.[1]

Or consider the ancient imagery comparing a human life to "the ship of Theseus." Suppose that over time, each and every one of a ship's planks gets replaced. As long as all of them aren't replaced at once—as long as the replacement is staggered, with some planks remaining on at any given time while adjacent ones change—it's the same ship at the end as at the beginning. Likewise with a human life. As long as there's never a moment when each and every one of a person's beliefs, hopes, thoughts, commitments, and memories are all replaced at a stroke—a catastrophic event that we would equate with total amnesia or utter personality breakdown—it will still be the same life, led by the same self, at the end as at the beginning. No matter how much complete turnover in beliefs, hopes, thoughts, commitments, and memories there is in the interim.

Is this true? It's a critical question when we think about the allure of immortality.

Bernard Williams says that an immortal life would eventually take one of two forms. It would be either interminably boring or else, in the final analysis, no different from a mortal one. Suppose, on the one hand, that as immortals all our memories, desires, habits, values, feelings, projects, attachments, and aspirations stayed with us endlessly over time, never trading themselves in for new ones.

We would, as millennia passed, ultimately reach a stage at which we'd have seen everything we cared to see and done all we cared to do. Our life would settle into an excruciating, insufferable, unending combination of ennui and lethargy. Catatonic boredom would be our fate.

On the other hand, Williams says, we could avoid such immortal boredom if—over time—we regularly lost our tired old memories, attachments, thoughts, aspirations, appetites, beliefs, and desires, replacing them with new ones. New things, things that we would find engaging, would continue to happen to us. We'd elude terminal boredom. But nor then would we really be immortal. After all, if we habitually shed all memory of our past experiences, perceptions, and thoughts—and if we ceased to harbor any interest at all in the aspirations, desires, and attachments that we used to have—then our old life would in effect have ended to make way for a new one. And that, of course, is what defines mortality, not immortality. We would no longer, Williams says, recognize ourselves in the new person we would eventually become. And so "he" might as well actually *be* a new person. Since we will have disappeared anyway, we might as well actually die.

Bone-crushing boredom—or else a kind of perpetual self-alienation, a kind of recurrent dying-to-oneself. That's the choice that Williams believes immortality offers us. Timothy Chappell nicely sums up the dilemma. If our life remains our own it "goes around in circles." And "if it doesn't go round in circles it ceases to be [our own]."[2]

Yet as the images of threads in a rope or planks in a boat suggest, mortal lives, even within themselves, already involve the continual replacement of the old with the new. Over time, we relinquish the memories of high-school shenanigans, romantic crushes, sporting pursuits, desire for Goth clothing, and ruminations inspired by the metaphysics classes of our youth, and eventually replace them with the attachment to our significant other, pursuit of pinochle, desire for argyle cardigans, and reveries inspired by the Maeve Binchy novels of our later years. Earlier versions of ourselves are always fading away, to be replaced by newer ones. In a normal mortal life, these turnovers in our memories, beliefs, attachments, pursuits, aspirations, and desires transpire in a staggered way, not all at once. Because there is no radical break, never a time when novelty in some areas of life isn't accompanied by persistence in others, we consider our early self and our later self to be the same one — even if the memories, desires, habits, beliefs, attachments, and aspirations we harbor toward the end of our life bear absolutely no resemblance to those we had when we were just starting out. We wouldn't ever think that we have died several times while still alive.

Why, then, shouldn't we view an immortal life — one that escaped boredom by jettisoning old memories, feelings, plans, values, and desires in a staggered way over time and replacing them with wholly new ones — in the same light? Why shouldn't an immortal self, no matter how wholly different it becomes over time, still be deemed one and the same continuing self as long as its changes don't all take place at the same abrupt moment? Even as mortals we do "not have a single, consistent life," Chateaubriand observes; we have "several . . . there is always a time when we possessed nothing of what we now possess, and a time when we [will] have nothing of what we once had."[3] Perhaps not all of us follow this pattern, but the point is that we would still consider a person who did completely change his memories, feelings, plans, desires, attachments, and thoughts over his life to be the same self, as long as the changes were staggered. Why, then, should Williams think that an immortal version of this process would have to entail the recurrent death of the self?

True, we consider a rope that completely changes its fibers over its length to still remain the same rope, as long as the changes are staggered. Likewise with a ship that completely changes its planks over its life. But think about fibers and planks. There's a vegetational, a still life, imagery going on here. Does it really capture a human self, a human life?

To address this question I'm going to explore a version of an idea that Derek Parfit floats. It's reasonable to think that I remain the same self today as I was yesterday—or the same "person," for Parfit—if at least half of the memories, desires, intentions, experiences, perceptions, plans, feelings, and beliefs that crossed my conscious mind yesterday also do so today.[4] As long as half continue on from one day to the next, half can change. Today, for example, I completed the memo I was working on yesterday, continued an e-mail exchange with my daughter that began yesterday, and recalled a conversation about garbage collection I had with my neighbor yesterday—but I also read a *Times* article by Paul Krugman, heard a joke about former Toronto mayor Rob Ford on *The Daily Show*, and had a Greek salad for lunch: none of which occurred yesterday.

As long as I keep on mutating in this staggered way day by day, then I can remain the same self I was twenty years ago, even if all my daily memories, desires, beliefs, perceptions, and intentions then were utterly different. And if this works for me as a mortal self, why wouldn't it if I were immortal? Why couldn't I also remain the same self as I was 100,000 years previously, even if all my memories, desires, feelings, perceptions, and commitments then were wholly different—as long as, from any one day to the next in the interim, at least half of them continued to remain the same?

But why from one day to the next? Why not say that as long as half of our memories, commitments, feelings, aspirations, and desires continue from one five-second period to the next, then even if half change we will still remain the same person?

Presumably because, once we get to small enough units of time, there really is only one memory, desire, perception, feeling, or thought present during any given (say, five-second) period. In any given five-second span I can focus only on the memo I am working on, or on the e-mail to my daughter, or on *The Daily Show* joke, or on Krugman's *Times* article, or on the Greek salad, or on the remembered neighborly conversation about garbage pickup. The next five seconds will contain either the same or a completely different mental event. When units of time are very brief, there simply aren't enough distinct memories, desires, feelings, perceptions, or thoughts in each to speak of "half" continuing on to the next.

Let's go then from very short to very long periods of time. Why not say that as long as half of our memories, desires, perceptions, feelings, aspirations, and thoughts continue from one year to the next, half can change and we will still remain the same self? I assume it's for this reason: of all the distinct memories, desires, intentions, perceptions, sensations, and thoughts that enter our mind in any given year, far less than half will ever enter our mind in the next year. Next year—given the pace of life—I won't be recalling the same exchanges with the neighbor, continuing the same e-mail discussion with my daughter, or (God willing) working on the same memos I was this year, let alone reading the same *Times* articles or hearing the same topical *Daily Show* jokes—although I almost certainly will have many of this year's lunches.

So if seconds are too short, and years are too long, then a day suggests itself as the right unit—a unit over which at least half of my memories, desires, intentions, perceptions, and thoughts can reasonably be expected to continue from one to the next, and, if they do, it would be reasonable to consider me the same continuing self.

And yet there's a problem with this day-to-day approach.

Suppose, for the sake of simplicity, that only six feelings, experiences, memories, thoughts, and the like cross a person's mind on any given day. And suppose that on Monday, mine were the following: I had fond thoughts of my wife. I walked the dog. I experienced the feeling of anxiety about nothing in particular that I do more days than not. I felt satisfaction, given my concerns about climate change, that the world's governments seemed to be inching toward some kind of concord. I worked on my book about mortality. I enjoyed the many levels of irony in a story a colleague told me.

On Tuesday, I continued to have loving thoughts about my wife. I again walked the dog. And I persisted in experiencing the usual vague anxiousness that I did on Monday. But for whatever reason,

I permanently abandoned the concerns about climate change I held on Monday and for decades previously, replacing them with an avid yearning to see Ted Cruz elected president. I irrevocably gave up working on mortality, superseding that activity with a new career writing children's stories. And I forever lost my sense of irony, supplanting it with a dead earnestness.

Wednesday then rolls around. I continue to support Ted Cruz, write children's stories, and maintain a deadly earnestness as I began to do for the first time on Tuesday. But I now also permanently cease doing everything I carried over to Tuesday from Monday. I quit having loving thoughts about my wife, replacing them with a desire to become a Benedictine monk. I resolve never again to walk the dog and, in lieu, take up daily naps. And I forever lose my free-floating anxiety and become instead reliably cheerful.

Over the period from Monday to Wednesday, half of my memories, desires, feelings, perceptions, and thoughts continued on from one day to the next in staggered fashion. But most of us would reject the claim that I am any more the same self, or am leading the same life, on Wednesday as I was on Monday. If everything permanently changes in the space essentially of one day, Tuesday, doesn't that amount to a total rupture of the sort we associate with blanket amnesia or other kinds of dramatic personality breakdown?

All of which suggests that there's something fundamentally misconceived about the entire enterprise of analogizing a person's memories, desires, thoughts, hopes, commitments, aspirations, attachments, and perceptions to a rope's fibers or a ship's planks. We might think that as long as those memories, thoughts, hopes, and perceptions change in staggered fashion—half, say, remaining the same while half change during any given period of time—then even if all of them eventually completely turned over to forestall boredom we'd remain the same self.

But in practical terms there's no unit of time—seconds, days, years—over which this would work. Either there aren't enough memories, desires, intentions, perceptions, and so forth to speak of "half" of them in the first place, as when the unit is small, like seconds. Or there are enough but far less than half of them would survive from one unit to the next, as when that unit is large, like years. Or else, as with days, there are enough memories, perceptions, thoughts, and feelings *and* half of them might reasonably be expected to survive from one to the next—but then total turnover could occur within a space of time, a single day, far too brief to be called "staggered."

So let's set aside, for the moment, the question of whether any particular adjacent periods in our life—be they seconds, days, or years—share at least half of their memories, desires, beliefs, feelings, experiences, and plans. Let's consider, instead, a different question: whether any particular memories, desires, beliefs, feelings, experiences, and plans repeatedly occur in at least half of the periods—be they days, months, or years—over most of our life. What keeps me the same person over time might simply be that, in half or more of my days or months or years, from childhood to old age, the same small number of memories, thoughts, feelings, attachments, and desires recurrently cross my consciousness: regardless of whether most of the rest fail to make it even from one day, let alone month or year, to the next.

Think of Molly's early morning reflections as she lies in bed next to Bloom in *Ulysses*. Far more than half of the thoughts, feelings, memories, plans, and sensations that wash across her mind probably won't survive even till the following dawn: a semiconscious thought of people getting up in China as her alarm rings; her plans to buy flowers at Lambes. But a select few number among those she undoubtedly does have on most of the days of her life—and certainly countless times every single year: memories of the men who were interested in her in the past, or her frustrated desires for a career as a singer. Google the phrase "there isn't a day that goes by when I don't think of [X]," and see what you get. It is these that make her—and us—a continuing self.

Or what about Claude Sylvanshine, the hapless IRS official from David Foster Wallace's *Pale King?* Sitting on a Chicago–Peoria flight,

Sylvanshine contemplates the seat number on his armrest, a mental event he never had before nor ever will again, even within that day. Most of the thoughts, perceptions, feelings, and intentions that cross his mind during the trip fall into that category. But a certain few are ones he has every year, many, many times, and probably most days, so that they become the stitches that knit his psychological life together. Like the feeling of impending terror that Claude has come to imagine in the form of a predatory bird. These kinds of relatively few but persistent memories, thoughts, hopes, and feelings are what make us the same self over the course of our life. Our self gradually emerges as they do in our early years. And it then gradually disappears with them during the mental ravages of old age.

The idea that Parfit floats is a short-term quantitative one. We examine all the separate memories, desires, thoughts, plans, perceptions, and feelings that cross our mind today, and all the ones that did yesterday, and if half are similar then we remain the same self on this day as we were on the previous one. And we will continue to remain the same self for as long as this criterion is met.

But what if, in reality, far more than half—Molly's drowsy image of people getting up in China, Sylvanshine's momentary glimpse of the number on his armrest—don't even last beyond the day? More important, what about the far less than half—Molly's desire to sing, or Sylvanshine's thoughts of the terrifying bird of prey—that cross our mind during far more than half of our days for decades? And what about those few that cross our mind if not on most days then at least once a month, like Bernstein's memory, in *Citizen Kane*, of the girl he had seen on the ferry years before ("I'll bet a month hasn't gone by since that I haven't thought of that girl"). Shouldn't the long-term, qualitative importance of those fewer but far more persistent memories, thoughts, feelings, sensations, and intentions not ultimately be determinant as to whether our self persists over time—and when it ends?

But if they are, then we run smack into Bernard Williams's dilemma.

For it's precisely such memories, plans, feelings, thoughts, perceptions, and desires—the comparatively small number that enter our mind consistently, and perhaps more days than not, year in and year out—that would eventually have to be abandoned if we are to avoid immortal boredom. After all, if anything becomes boring over endless time, it will be those memories, aspirations, attachments, experiences, and emotions that become most familiar and repetitious. If anything, it will be his thinking about the bird of prey every single day for endless thousands of years that will sooner or later render Sylvanshine exquisitely tired of himself, just as dwelling ad nauseum on her frustrated desire to be a singer will for Molly. But then, if that same recurrent drumbeat of a particular few memories, beliefs, thoughts, plans, and desires are the ones that define the self—and if they are also what must be shaken off in order to avoid immortal boredom—the self they defined will go with them. Would Sylvanshine be Sylvanshine without the bird of prey? Or Molly be Molly without her desire to sing? Parts of their selves would have disappeared.

So it looks as if it might be Williams's immortal choice—boredom or eventual death in life—after all.

Fibers overlapping in a rope. Or planks getting replaced in a staggered fashion on a ship. Let's look more closely at these fiber and plank metaphors—metaphors for the memories, desires, perceptions, sensations, and other mental contents that make up our life.

A rope, as it extends in space, can indeed be made up of separate fibers that begin and end in staggered fashion. Over space, it can remain the same rope at the beginning as at the end, even if no fibers remain the same throughout. But what about over time? Do new fibers get added to a rope in staggered fashion as old ones fray and crumble? No. Maybe a few tufts get lost here or there. But the rope's main fibers last as long as the rope does—in time, if not in space. And once those fibers are gone, so is the rope. It's the same rope at the beginning as at the end of its existence only if some fibers—in fact most—remain the same throughout.

Likewise with the planks in a ship. Certainly, they might be staggered in space. Think of the boards on a ship's deck. They don't all begin and end at the same line any more than the boards do in your living-room floor. Over its length, it remains the same ship even if none of the planks at the stern are the same as the ones at the bow. But can a ship change all its planks in staggered fashion over time, as the ship of Theseus metaphor requires, while remaining the same vessel? No. Sure, some—maybe most—pieces of wood in the decks or cabins or masts might get replaced, possibly on several occasions, over time. But a ship's broad structural beams? Its oaken hull strut? Those remain the same for the life of the ship. The one part of a ship that never gets replaced is its structural keel; if it breaks, the ship dies. A new keel means a new ship. It lasts for as long as the ship does, and in fact defines how long the ship lasts.[5]

Ropes and ships, it turns out, furnish inapt metaphors if what they're meant to show is that a self can change all of its memories, desires, beliefs, anxieties, plans, and feelings over time and still remain the same as long as those changes are staggered. For in fact at least some components of a rope or a ship—most of its fibers and certain of its planks—must persist in time, even if not in space, for as long as the rope or ship itself does. And once they are gone, so is the rope or ship. If anything, these metaphors reinforce the idea that it is our most persistent, recurrent memories, feelings, thoughts, experiences, and desires that define the self. And once we completely replace them even if in a staggered fashion—as immortals would ultimately have to do to avoid interminable boredom—then the self they constituted would have died.

So let's consider a truly temporal metaphor that purports to capture the idea that a human being can shed all her memories, desires, beliefs, plans, and attachments, replacing them with new ones—and yet remain the same self—as long as the shedding and replacing has been staggered over time.

Think about the husbands and wives in the Van Tricasse family, from Jules Verne's novella *Dr. Ox's Experiment.* Beginning in the

year 1340, each time one spouse dies the surviving partner immediately marries someone much younger. On any given day over the
subsequent centuries, at least one of the two spouses is the same as on
the day before, even though neither of the partners in 1440, let alone
1840, is the same as he or she was in 1340. There is always continuity, never any total break. The Van Tricasses believed that this ar-
rangement constituted the same marriage extending over hundreds
of years, not simply recurrent generations of new people replacing
old ones.

This is the acid test. If you agree with the Van Tricasses, then you'd
agree that a person can remain the same self over time, even if all her
memories, desires, feelings, perceptions, and intentions are totally
different, as long as the changes have been staggered. But most of
us, I think, would not regard this as the same marriage over time.
It's a series of new ones. Wholly new people, even if they're "staggered," make it a new one. Likewise, wholly new memories, desires,
intentions, plans, and beliefs, even if they're staggered, make a new
person. To truly avoid immortal boredom, it would seem, we must
die—one way or another.

If the self is like a rope, then it's like a rope in time, not in space.
Some memories, hopes, plans, imaginings, feelings, and desires must
remain the same over the self's entire temporal life if it's to persist
as the same self—just as some fibers in a rope must remain the same
over its entire temporal life, even if not over its entire spatial length,
if it's to persist as the same rope. But that suggests that an immortal
life, if it is to elude the sameness of memory, plans, hopes, ambitions,
feelings, experiences, and desires that over millennia would lead to
excruciating boredom, would eventually have to involve its own form
of death: an utter alienation from and desertion of previous selves,
and the memories, plans, desires, and attachments—all the mental
contents—that defined them. Ultimately immortality would be no
better than mortality. Bernard Williams's consolation has validity.[6]

eleven

A WISTFUL BACKWARD GLANCE

Nostalgia, as Simone Signoret remarked in her 1976 autobiography, isn't what it used to be. Each new generation yearns for the high water mark of the previous one. Woody Allen played with this theme in *Midnight in Paris*. A contemporary American writer longs for the Jazz Age literary scene, to which he then finds himself magically transported, only to fall in love with a flapper nostalgic for the 1890s Belle Epoque, to which they then miraculously travel, only to then encounter Degas, Gauguin, and Toulouse-Lautrec, all nostalgic for a still earlier age, and so on. Nostalgia, in this sense, never is—or ever could be—what it used to be.

But there's another sense in which nostalgia isn't what it used to be. As we in the early twenty-first century think of it, nostalgia is a temporal notion. It means, colloquially, a longing for a lost time, a time we have left behind. But it used to be—in fact it originated as—a spatial notion, a longing for a lost place, a home we have left behind. When the word "nostalgia" was minted in the eighteenth century, the historian Thomas Dodman reports, it "differed from subsequent forms of 'nostalgia' by its spatial as opposed to temporal construction."[1] As late as 1949, the *New York Times* was flatly asserting that "nostalgia means 'homesickness'—nothing more, nothing less. The word [comes] from the Greek nostos, 'a return home,' plus algia, 'pain.'"[2]

This point needs a bit of adjustment. Even when it carried spatial connotations—an aching for a lost home—nostalgia necessarily conveyed as well a temporal meaning. After all, to move away from home logically entails transit not just in space but in time. Emigrés pining for the warm embrace of the youth they spent in the old country are missing something that is now distant not just in miles but in years. The author of a 1935 *Washington Post* article,

Theodore Hall, captured this mixed spatial-temporal yearning when he spoke of his "homesickness for the old days in America."[3] Hall was referring to his generation of farm boys who had flooded America's teeming cities in the early years of the twentieth century, only to find themselves tearily nostalgic decades later for what they had left behind—left behind both in space and in time. So spatial nostalgia almost always has a temporal dimension.

According to the philosopher Hans Jonas, an immortal life would instill in those living it a lengthening, deepening, and finally intolerable—and of course interminable—nostalgia: but it would be a nostalgia of a purely temporal sort, a longing for an eternally receding past. It's a scenario for immortality that splits the difference between those discussed in the previous two chapters: boredom, on the one hand, and recurrent self-alienation on the other.

The boredom scenario would arise if, in an immortal existence, both our self and our lives ceased to change. Suppose that the memories, commitments, values, desires, thoughts, feelings, and anxieties that make up our original self all stayed with us as we moved forward endlessly in time. And imagine that the events of our lives, continually flowing through our fingers backward in time, all began to repeat themselves as the millennia passed. At one point we would have seen it all, done all we cared to do, and nothing new would ever seem to happen.

The self-alienation scenario, equally unpalatable, would emerge from the opposite situation. Suppose that our immortal selves did keep shedding our old memories, desires, commitments, beliefs, habits, and aspirations, replacing them with new ones. And suppose, too, that our endless lives did continue to throw novel and unprecedented events at us. True, we wouldn't be bored. We'd continue to experience and do new things. But then we'd also undergo a recurrent alienation from our past selves and lives. Our old selves and lives would in effect keep ending to make way for new ones. And that, of course, is what defines mortality, not immortality.

The third immortality scenario, the one that transfixes Hans Jonas, combines aspects of these other two. It would descend on immortals whose memories, values, commitments, passions, desires, and habits did remain the same over the ages (so no self-alienation), but whose lives nevertheless still regularly presented them with new events and unprecedented challenges (so no boredom). Unfortunately, such an existence would induce a crushing nostalgia as time passed.

Why? Even for us mortals, Jonas says, the past "grows in us all the time, with its load of knowledge and opinion and emotions and choices and acquired aptitudes and habits and, of course, things upon things remembered." Given the growing weight of the past within us—our memories, feelings, aptitudes and habits—suppose, then, that we were immortal, but faced a future of unending upheaval and change. And why wouldn't we, Jonas asks, since generations of "new comers [would] keep arriving" over the ages with their never-before-seen ideas, talents, desires, and tastes. Sooner or later wouldn't we find ourselves "stranded," as Jonas says, "in a world we no longer [understood] even as spectators, walking anachronisms who have outlived themselves?"[4] Wouldn't we pine for the ever-more-distant past, which long ago captured our memories, formed our desires, shaped our habits, and forged our emotional attachments, fruitlessly yearning for it to return?

Jonas seals his case by calling himself as a witness. While he "can still be moved" when he remembers the culture of his youth in Weimar Rhineland, a culture that awakened his passions and tastes, Jonas—now in his eighties—declares that

> the art of our own time is alien to me, I don't understand its language, and in that respect I feel already a stranger in the world. The prospect of unendingly becoming one ever more and in every respect would be frightening, and the certainty that prevents it is reassuring.[5]

Such would be the fate of any immortal, if her memory, feelings, habits, passions and beliefs retained ever-more white-knuckled attachments to an ever-receding past, while she confronted an unendingly churning and novel future.

Or would it? After all, profound nostalgia—of the mixed spatial-temporal sort—has marked innumerable worthwhile and intensely rich mortal lives. Think of the exiled Nabokov's lifelong yearnings for Vyra, his family's estate outside Saint Petersburg. Or Samad Iqbal's mournful backward glances at Bangladesh in Zadie Smith's *White Teeth*. Or the memoirist Suketu Mehta, finding himself "in one city" while "dreaming of the other . . . an exile; [a] citizen of the country of longing."[6]

All leave their familial and familiar childhood homes for strange new places—thus lending their yearning its fundamentally spatial character—where they then spend the coming years, compounding that spatial longing with a temporal dimension. Such nostalgia-drenched mortal lives, though, can be profoundly livable and ful-filling. They can be endurable and enriching precisely because of that nostalgia, that evocative longing and exquisite yearning, which can mature into great humanity, passion, and art. Why, then, should Jonas think that nostalgia would render immortal life intolerable, and hence worse than the alternative?

But what if the nostalgia that would grind away at us in immortal life differs from the bittersweet, resonant type that infuses the humanly warm mortal lives of a Nabokov or a Mehta? What if it's the spatial dimension of their longings, a yearning for a former place—not for a former time—that lends mortal nostalgia whatever deeply redeeming humanity it possesses? If so, then can the purely temporal nostalgia, the nostalgia for an ever-receding past that Jonas envisions for immortals, ever nurture the same redemptive richness?

Think of the spatial element of nostalgia. Think of the émigré's pining for home. And think of his feeling like a stranger, even an intruder, in his new land: like a "newcomer, an outsider, the one who did not belong," as the uprooted Malinalli reflects in Laura Esquivel's *Malinche*.[7] While the émigré with spatial nostalgia feels like a newcomer, courting resentment from those long-timers who believe that he has invaded their world, the immortal with purely temporal nostalgia undergoes a very different experience. He feels *himself* to be the long-timer, and it is his world that is being invaded by (as Jonas says) "newcomers who keep arriving": youngsters with their new music, their new art, their new technology; their new social codes and cues; their new ruthlessness and recklessness.

So yes, a person with purely temporal nostalgia has traveled far from the olden days for which he yearns, just like the person with spatial nostalgia has traveled far from the old country for which he pines. But instead of feeling like an arriviste in the new era, the temporal nostalgic is the one who feels besieged by new arrivals. He feels himself not so much an intruder as intruded upon.

What this means is that while those who are spatially nostalgic might feel unsettled, those who are temporally nostalgic risk becoming unhinged. Certainly it can be disorienting to move to a new land, as the spatial nostalgic has done. But at least he is the one who has done the moving; the spatial world itself remains stationary. Not only that but the old country and the new remain at a fixed, bridgeable distance from each other. This isn't the case, though, for those who are temporally nostalgic. It's not they who have moved to a new temporal world. Instead, a "new world is [always] coming quickly" toward them, "a harsh, cruel world" of new ideas and mores and expectations, as Madame observes in Kazuo Ishiguro's *Never Let Me Go*.[8] Temporal nostalgics are the ones who are stuck while the world—the world of time, not space—is in dizzying, hurtling, unending motion, driving the old and the new ever further and further away from each other as (assuming immortality) the centuries endlessly mount. Not just disorienting, but dismembering: pulling the self apart.

But there's something more. In Kiran Desai's *Inheritance of Loss*, Biju, a young man marooned in fast-food jobs around New York City, longs for his west Bengali village. Yet while the spatially nostalgic Biju wishes that he himself as an individual could cross the ocean back to the Bengal, he doesn't want the entire city of New York to move back with him, rolling across the sea to India.

Now, though, think of the temporally nostalgic Hans Jonas. His situation is the reverse. What he doesn't want is to go back in time to the 1920s himself, as an individual. He doesn't aspire to be younger, to be the child he once was. What he would want is for the current time, itself, to go backward: that the whole present age, its culture and politics, its religion and science, all roll back to the era he loved most, the time of his youth. The only thing that would satisfy his yearning, were it possible, is that styles of music, cinema, dance, clothing, architecture, visual art, literature, and everything else unwind in time from the 1980s and '90s, in which he spent his later years, to those of the Weimar era. What Jonas would want is a return to a public past time, a past that everyone shared, a past with a different style, feel, sensibility, intelligence, and understanding than the present.

A spatially imbued nostalgia, by contrast, precludes the need for any such impossibly gargantuan wish. True, a desire to return to the place of our youth may well dovetail with a desire to return to a *personal* past time, the time one enjoyed—the sounds, the fragrances, the warm embraces—that one experienced there as a child: what Hilton Als, mixing the spatial and the temporal, calls "the old country of childhood."[9] And yes, when spatial nostalgia drives temporal nostalgia along this personal path—when the "longing for home," as Svetlana Boym puts it, gets "shrunk to the longing for one's own childhood"[10]—then that kind of temporal nostalgia can be rich and resonant, redolent with warm glows and wistful glistenings.

But without spatial longing lending it a personal coloring, temporal nostalgia becomes cold and bereft. When the author Simon Reynolds observes that to "exist in Time is to suffer through an endless exile, a successive severing from those precious few moments of feeling at home in the world," he is describing something totally immiserating, because it's a yearning that can never be requited.[11] You can't go back in time as you can in space. And, unlike the distance back in space, the distance back in time grows greater moment by moment.

Churchill's funeral took place at St. Paul's Cathedral on January 30, 1965. The journalist Bernard Levin, in his history of Britain in the 1960s, describes one of the more memorable photographs taken that day. It featured the eighty-two-year-old former Labour prime minister Clement Attlee—who had defeated Churchill in 1945 only to be defeated in turn by Churchill in 1951—waiting to be picked up following the ceremony. Attlee, Levin writes, "was accommodated on the steps of the cathedral with a simple wooden chair, and sat there, bowed over his stick, remembering."[12]

If immortal life takes the path that Jonas predicts, that image captures those who will have to live it. While the spatially nostalgic émigré is the one who moves to a new world, and in principle can always move back to the old one, the temporally nostalgic immortal keeps getting besieged by new worlds moving at him and pines, in vain, to bring back the old one. And so immortal nostalgia would be far worse than the mortal kind. Hans Jonas's "nostalgia" consolation for mortality has validity.

The philosopher Martha Nussbaum finds immortality appealing. "As I imagine successive careers for myself (as a cantor, an actress, a psychoanalyst, a novelist)" over endless time, Nussbaum writes, there'd be sufficient change to stave off boredom. But not so much change that she'd entirely cease to be Martha Nussbaum: that she herself would disappear. "I have no difficulty imagining that I would be recognizably myself in all" these new adventures, Nussbaum writes, since "all these pursuits [would be] done in a Martha-ish way."[1]

I have to wonder, though. If her Martha-ishness means anything, from my sense of Prof. Nussbaum, it's that she has a distinctive personality rooted in (among other things) a love of the ancient world, of opera, and of the magnificent ruin that is the aging human body, as well as deep allegiances to feminism and social justice. In other words, her Martha-ishness is planted in a very particular set of times, both present and past.

Meanwhile the successive careers that the world offered her would sooner or later mutate beyond recognition. Cantor, psychoanalyst, actress, and novelist are, as human endeavors, already under siege, at least in their traditional forms, thanks to innovations in religious observance, breakthroughs in pharmaceuticals, developments in computer animation, and upheavals in internet self-publishing. Those pursuits seem unlikely to persist over decades, let alone centuries or millennia, in any form that Nussbaum or the rest of us can presently foresee or would even recognize.

So I wonder. Wouldn't the kind of groundedness in the past, the kind of Martha-ishness necessary to keep Nussbaum the same person over time on the one hand, and the kind of changes the world would throw at her so that she could evade boredom on the other hand, not conspire to make her feel increasingly, interminably nostalgic as centuries and millennia passed? Like Hans Jonas's stranger in an ever stranger land?

Or look at it this way: sure, from any one decade to the next, continuity in memory, feelings, beliefs, habits, characteristics, aspirations and desires—my Andrew-ishness, if I can borrow from Nussbaum—might make for a persisting self, thus warding off self-alienation. But as those decades ceaselessly pile up, and one decade of the same memories, feelings, beliefs, habits, characteristics, aspirations, and desires gets added on top of the previous ones ad infinitum, that continuity would become a recipe for paralytic boredom.

And sure, from any one decade to the next, a change in career might ward off boredom. But as those decades endlessly pile up, and one change compounds the previous one, which compounded the previous one, and so forth, such changes would, in toto, become a road map to the death of previous selves, to profound self-alienation.

Boredom, self-alienation, and nostalgia each have their mortal equivalents. And some of those mortal versions can be livable, perhaps tolerable, possibly even valuable, or at least preferable to death. We should be under no illusions, though—as I have tried to suggest—that their immortal variants would be so benign.

But something in me, perhaps in you too, rebels at these dire prognoses. Is there no "play in the joints" here, no immortal path that can somehow slip betwixt and between these grim scenarios? In pursuing this question, we will necessarily encounter some of the more fantastic and speculative projections for immortality that mortal minds have generated.

They Can't Take That Away from You—But on the Other Hand, You Can't Take It with You

Think of a stereotypical view—and for simplicity's sake, I take as an example a stereotypical adolescent male heterosexual view although it can easily be adapted for any set of preferences—of what a blissful immortality might look like. You're in love with Barbara Ann. But you're also intrigued by Betty Lou, Peggy Sue, Mary Lou, and countless others. If you were immortal, you could regularly delight in Barbara Ann's company over the course of thousands of millennia, while enjoying short affairs with Betty, Peggy, Mary, and the unending others who catch your eye. You wouldn't get nostalgic about Barbara Ann because you'd always be able to spend time with her—she's not going anywhere. But you wouldn't get bored either, because there are so many alternatives. Nor would you become self-alienated, an aimless drifter: your innumerable encounters with Barbara Ann would maintain a heft, a continuity, a mooring of deep intimacy in your romantic life throughout all the exciting changes it undergoes—forever.

You can substitute men, careers, hobbies, food, drink, mystical experiences, voyages to different galaxies, or anything else you like for Barbara Ann and company. Immortality seems just fine.

But there's another way of looking at it.

Unless you are Mick Jagger, you will know how many lovers you have had. But unless you are Miles Monroe, Woody Allen's character from the movie *Sleeper*—"Sex and death: two things that come once in a lifetime"—you will not know how many times you've made love. You will know how many lovers you've had because in counting them, you—as we all do when we tote up different kinds of notches on our belt—treat your partners as objects to be accumulated. You won't know how many times you've made love, though, because you treat those moments not as objects but as the experiences they are, enjoying them as they happen and then letting them slip through your fingers back into the past.

That's not set in stone. Fiction and real life furnish instances of people who add up and record in their diaries as if they were objects to be stockpiled, with commentary on each episode, their individual sexual experiences.[2] The good things in life, many of them, lend themselves to being treated either as objects or as experiences; within bounds the choice is yours.

But here's the rub: it would seem as if immortality looks more appealing to the extent that we think of its contents as objects, not experiences. If you are bored with an object (Mary Lou, Peggy Sue, Betty Lou), you can always give it up or slip away from it. If you are feeling nostalgic for an object (Barbara Ann) you can always go and visit it, or simply keep it perpetually with you. And no need to worry about self-alienation. You can always seek out new objects (Mary, Peggy, Betty) while keeping the old—Barbara Ann, that continuing touchstone in your life—close at hand. If we imagine an immortal paradise, this is likely be our implicit model, and whatever we view as an object will qualify.

But experiences? Here are three lessons, drawn from the master, Proust, about experiences. First, you can't take them with you the way you can an object. As soon as they happen they begin falling back in time as you forge ahead. Maybe you can always go and revisit Barbara Ann the person. But you can't revive Barbara Ann the experience. You can't keep that with you to revel in at will. Over time, she will have changed, as will you. Nostalgia seems foreordained.[3]

Second, while you can't take an experience with you, in another sense no one can take an experience away from you. Those moments you had with Mary Lou or Peggy Sue or Betty Lou? Once having happened they can't unhappen. You can't cleanse your own personal past of an experience that no longer pleases you, in the way that you can clear your own personal space of an object that no longer delights you. Nor can you speed through time away from an experience as soon as it becomes tiresome, in the way that you can speed through space away from an object as soon as it becomes irksome. Your encounter with any new Mary, or Peggy, or Betty will inevitably unfold under a shadow: a shadow cast by the doldrums in which all the previous ones—no matter how exciting they were to begin with—ultimately ended. Boredom, sooner or later, seems foreordained.[4]

And finally, not being tangible in the way that objects are, experiences blur into each other. Even though you've had innumerable passionate embraces with Barbara Ann, that central thread in your life who keeps you the same person, only a handful will ever remain in your mind as significant. Perhaps they will meld into just one composite, blurred, and fragmentary memory. For that reason, accumulating experiences will always seem more pointless than accumulating objects. All the moments you spent with Barbara Ann will begin collapsing into themselves. Over a long enough time, they will scarcely have the heft to provide the backbone for an ongoing sense of self. Over a long enough time, self-alienation always threatens.[5]

Certainly, if immortality meant moving through endless space instead of through endless time, then our capacities to retain, scrap, or accumulate objects at will might legitimately be the dominant template in our psychology. But immortality doesn't mean moving in endless space with respect to objects. It means moving in endless time with respect to experiences. Treating irretrievable experiences as if we could retain them like objects, or irreversible experiences as if we could scrap them like objects, or blurry experiences as if we could accumulate them like objects, will be less and less possible as time passes. And unfortunately their irretrievability guarantees nostalgia. Their irreversibility augurs boredom. Their blurriness portends self-alienation. In the end the "Barbara Ann" scenario fails to bar nostalgia, boredom, and self-alienation from awaiting us as different versions of our immortal fate.

Robert Ettinger, the mind behind the cryonics movement, seems to me to have bought into the Barbara Ann scenario. Cryonics technology enables us to have our head or entire body frozen just before or after death, on the assumption that in the centuries ahead, when medical science is able to cure the disease to which we succumbed, someone will thaw us out and we will resume living. Perhaps we will even live forever, if the thawing takes place at a time when humankind has discovered the secret to immortality. Paradise awaits.

I say, though, that Ettinger bought into the Barbara Ann scenario because, in addition to having had himself frozen when he died in 2011, he had previously frozen both of the two wives he outlived. He intended them all to be defrosted when the time came. For Ettinger, it would seem, his two wives weren't experiences that, as he looked forward to an immortal future, he was willing to let drift back into the past. They were objects to be accumulated.

I foresee trouble in paradise.

Slow It Down

Here's another scenario for a possibly blissful immortality. Most of us, over the course of our mortal lives, gradually forget most of our memories and replace many of our desires: we exchange the memories and desires of our childhood for those of adolescence, then adulthood, then old age. Shedding our memories and shifting our desires help keep the world fresh and so allow us to dodge overwhelming boredom. Acquiring new memories and developing new desires also enable us to stay engaged in the present and so evade crushing nostalgia for earlier times. But we never overhaul our memories or our desires so completely that we lose the thread of our self and become someone else entirely. We somehow manage to elude recurrent self-alienation.

What's more, most of us face a future whose events contain enough novelty to allow us to cheat boredom. But those events are rarely so wholly unprecedented that we risk becoming anachronisms in our own lifetime, hence suffering debilitating nostalgia. Nor are they so wholly unprecedented that we risk becoming strangers to our former selves, hence undergoing rupturing self-alienation. Most of us, then, over the course of our mortal life become neither cripplingly bored nor desperately nostalgic nor deeply self-alienated. Why couldn't immortal life be like that?

Perhaps it could. But for a life that lasted eons to stand a chance of unfolding in such a fashion, everything would have to scale up accordingly.

Think of the lover in Andrew Marvell's famous poem of seduction. If his mistress and he were immortal, the lover says, then the two of them would have all the time in the world to luxuriate in teasing and titillating each other.

> An hundred years should go to praise
> Thine eyes, and on thy forehead gaze;
> Two hundred to adore each breast,
> But thirty thousand to the rest

Caressing his mistress's breasts every night for eternity, the lover seems to realize, would risk becoming tedious. He'd have to spread things out a bit, say a caressing once every fifty thousand years, to avoid boredom. But if after fifty thousand years the caressing then lasted for the current mortal norm of only (say) fifteen minutes, it wouldn't have sufficient weight in the lover's experience to combat nostalgia for caresses past. Nor would it have enough substance to form an ongoing and significant thread in his life, warding off self-alienation. That's why, as the lover says, a proper caress should take two hundred years. A mere quarter of an hour, and it would be such a small pinpoint in an immortal life that it would fail to satisfy any nostalgia for previous moments of intimacy or assume the role of a meaningful, self-constituting event.

So for us to avoid boredom, nostalgia, and self-alienation, everything in our immortal life would have to lengthen in time accordingly, the caressing of breasts and all else in the intervals in between. We would live the same lives as we do now, only in slow motion: just as Marvell's lover proposes.

But then if everything really did "slow down" proportionately, what would we have gained? As the philosopher Frank Arntzenius observes, "It does not make much sense to suppose that if everything in the world were to speed up uniformly it would change my mental state."[6] Likewise, presumably, if everything were to slow down uniformly. An immortal's experience of immortality, on this "slow it down" scenario, might elude paralytic boredom, rupturing self-alienation and intolerable nostalgia. But that's because it wouldn't differ from our experience of mortal life as it is.

Ramp It Up

In any case, this kind of immortal life—an unlimited life span that somehow contains the same number of events as a mortal life, with each event elongated accordingly, and which would feel effectively like a mortal life—is not on the table. So Marvell's lover proposes an intriguing alternative: yet another fantasy of immortality.

Take our limited life span as it is. And then radically ramp up the number of events it contains. Don't waste even a second. And in that way, by cramming into a mortal life all of the experiences you would get in an immortal life, you would feel as if you have lived one. This is what the lover means with his concluding proposal to his mistress: "Though we cannot make our sun stand still, yet we will make him run."

The sun—its rising and its setting—is what we use to mark the passage of the daily cycle. By "making the sun run," the lover and his mistress would simply speed that daily cycle up. They would, in other words, break the normal equation between the day as marked by the sun's rising and setting and the day as marked in another common way: by the passing of twenty-four hours. Lover and mistress would seek to pack more and more sunrise-to-sunset days into a twenty-four-hour day. That's what it means to make the sun run.

Of course, it's impossible to literally make the sun rise and set more quickly. The sun's run from morning to night is simply a metaphor for our everyday circuit of events. So instead of sunrise, think morning coffee. Instead of sunset, think evening nightcap. And then think of all the events in between, whether dallying with one's amour, carousing with one's friends, playing with one's children, jesting with one's colleagues, closing a corporate acquisition, or hiking a mountain trail. What the lover is saying is: ramp it up. Jam, say, seven of these coffee-dalliance-carousing-playing-jesting-closing-hiking-nightcap cycles—each representing a day's events—into a twenty-four-hour period. It will now take seven such coffee-to-nightcap days, instead of just one, for us to complete a twenty-four-hour day.

Then (so Marvell's lover asks) would we not in effect have slowed time down? Won't each single day now stretch out and feel like a week? Won't we have made our lives seem 700 percent longer?

Consider an analogy. Suppose that, instead of taking one day to travel two hundred and forty miles across the state, you decide to take seven days to do so. You will have slowed things down. The trip will last longer. Likewise, suppose that instead of taking one coffee-to-nightcap day to pass a twenty-four-hour day, lover and mistress now take seven coffee-to-nightcap days to do so. Haven't they slowed time down, at least as they experience it? Won't each twenty-four-hour day—and thus their mortal life—seem that much longer? And what if they ramp things up still further, packing seventy or seven hundred or seven thousand coffee-nightcap days into a twenty-four-hour day? Then will they not slow their mortal life down to the point where it will resemble an immortal one? It's a lovely thought, and one that many of us entertain: we can come closer to immortality the more we pack into our mortal lives.[7]

But of course that's not what will happen, as anyone knows who has tried to pack more and more events into a limited period of time. What happens is that things don't slow down. They speed up.

Think of certain kinds of vacations, such as a ski trip, or a holiday at Disney World with the kids. During such periods, the psychologist Douwe Draaisma observes, we often experience "quick days": twenty-four-hour days that do not slow down but fly by at the time. And they do so precisely because we *are* packing them with several normal days' worth of events.[8] What Marvell's lover proposes, namely making the sun run, thus won't—as he thinks—slow life down till it seems endless. It will speed life up till it seems like the blink of an eye. True, such a life will defeat boredom, nostalgia, and self-alienation, simply because it will go by in a flash. But it won't feel immortal. Just the opposite.

What's interesting, though, is the nature of the mistaken assumption that underlies the lover's proposition.

The lover relies on a false analogy. As hours are to miles, he reasons, so events are to days. The more hours it takes you to pass through a mile, the slower the journey goes. Likewise, the more events it takes you to pass through the day, the slower the day goes.

In fact, though, it is not hours—but objects—that are to miles what events are to days. The more objects you cram into a mile, the less space there is for any one of them. And the space itself seems ever tighter. In the same way, the more events you cram into a day, the less time it takes to go through any one of them. And the day itself seems ever briefer. Events are not time's units, such that the more we put into each day the longer that day will seem. No, events are time's contents, such that the more we pack into each day the quicker the pace of life becomes—and the shorter the day will seem.[9]

I think here of the courageous Chinese dissident Yang Zili, whom I once met, and a prison story he told me. Jailed for eight years because he launched a reading group with a few friends, Yang was incarcerated in a single room that housed a large number of prisoners, all of whom slept next to each other on a sizable wooden board. The chief prisoner and his assistant—appointed by the guards to govern the cell—apportioned half the board for just themselves and, erecting a divider, left the remaining half for all the rest, who, because of their number, had to sleep on their sides, crammed up against each other like sardines.

One day a new prisoner arrived. But there seemed to be no room for him unless the chief and his assistant relinquished some of their space. This they were not prepared to do. Instead, at bedtime the chief directed the new inmate to the other prisoners' side of the divider. He then instructed the newcomer to lie on top of two of the prisoners, parallel to them in the groove where their bodies met. And the chief then pounded him like a wedge till the new arrival squeezed between them.

The temporal equivalent of *that* spatial experience is what awaits us, if we make the sun run ever faster.[10]

Flow

One final optimistic scenario for immortality, which I will credit to the philosopher Nick Bostrom: assume that you are not only immortal, but also vastly more intelligent than you are now. If you are a superintelligent immortal, Bostrom says,

> each day is a joy . . . you play a certain new kind of game which combines [virtual-reality] artistic expression, dance, humor, interpersonal dynamics, and various novel faculties and the emergent phenomena they make possible. . . . When you are playing this game with your friends, you feel how every fibre of your body and mind is stretched to its limit in the most creative and imaginative way.[11]

A fine balance: You are stretched to the limit, rendered neither so slack that you lose interest nor so taut that you snap.

What Bostrom describes resembles what the psychologist Mihaly Csikszentmihalyi calls a state of "flow" or "optimal experience." In flow situations, Csikszentmihalyi says, we encounter challenges that are not so same-old/same-old as to numb us with boredom. But nor do those challenges lie so far beyond the pale of our experience as to make us nostalgic for something more familiar. And in this state of fine balance, Csikszentmihalyi tells us, the "sense of time disappears. You forget yourself . . . feeling so focused on the present that you lose track of time passing."[12] After all, you have no inclination to let your mind wander either to the past (you're not nostalgic) or to the future (you're not bored) or to yourself (and so any self-alienation is a nonissue). "Time seems to fall away" in flow, the psychologist Kendra Cherry says, and we experience "a loss of self-consciousness."[13] Csikszentmihalyi quotes a rock climber on this point. In flow, "you are so involved in what you are doing [that] you aren't thinking of yourself as separate from the immediate activity. . . . You don't see yourself as separate from what you are doing."[14]

To abide in such a permanent sweet spot, so focused on the moment that all thoughts of self and time disappear, may well be a happy circumstance. But it's not one compatible with what I am here taking to be a keynote of the human condition: the sense we very much have of both self and time and, in particular, of being selves moving ever forward in time. After all, it's precisely our selves who, moving second by second in time toward our deaths, cry out for a reprieve from mortality.

Now suppose that that reprieve is granted. Suppose that we became immortal. But suppose too that we also became superintelligent. Immersed (as Bostrom says) in the "joy" of flow, we would no longer have any sense of self or of time passing. Certainly then we would not *feel* immortal. To do that we would need a sense of our selves persisting on in time. And continuous flow precludes that sense. As Michael Frayn says in his novel *A Landing on the Sun*, the "pleasure" that comes from "complete absorption in some conceptual problem . . . was precisely . . . the loss of all sense of self."[15] But isn't the loss of self a kind of death?

Of course, superintelligent immortals could always periodically emerge from flow. But then immortality would not be the heaven that Bostrom conjures up. Combining change and continuity in just the right mixture, flow ensures that you are neither bored by too much continuity nor rendered nostalgic by too much change. If, though, we fail to combine the challenging and the familiar in just the right way, then instead of heaven we will get hell. David Foster Wallace understood this. Require "a fellow . . . to perform rote tasks just tricky enough to make him think, but still rote," Wallace warns, and then "just leave the man there to his mind's devices."[16] In other words, assign him tasks challenging enough to keep him awake but familiar enough to make him desperately want to go to sleep. And then see what misery—the furthest thing from the heaven promised by flow—results. And Wallace was not even talking about an immortal hell, only a mortal one.

For however long it could be sustained, endless superintelligent flow might well be idyllic. Superintelligent immortals would constantly be "in the moment." But that's because all concern with self and time, and in that sense the difference between immortality and mortality, would have become irrelevant to them.[17]

*

No one, of course, can say what immortality, or even the for-all-intents-and-purposes immortality of much greater longevity, would be like. What Joan Didion calls "magical thinking" applies as much when we imagine that mortal creatures like us are immortal as when we pretend that dead people are alive.

But given what little we know, one thing merits pondering. It does seem that each of the major benign scenarios for immortality ultimately relies on a fantastic assumption, whether about our selves or about the moments of our lives.

One benign immortality scenario assumes that we would no longer be selves who moved relentlessly forward in time. Instead, our self would turn into a kind of liquid, dissolving into time's flow, becoming simply whatever it is doing at the present moment. Absorbed totally in the present instant, we'd experience neither boredom—which comes from the accumulating weight of the past—nor nostalgia, which emerges from the unending strangeness of the future. Both would fall away in this scenario for a blissful immortality.

In another benign immortality scenario, the self would also cease moving forward in time. But in this case it would simply expand like an accordion to encompass any measure of time. Merely by slowing things down as much as necessary to match its ever-lengthening life span—taking a hundred years to gaze upon a forehead or two hundred to adore a breast—an immortal self could remain just as coherent as a mortal one.

Another benign immortality scenario needs to assume that the experiences of our lives would no longer slip, moment by moment, relentlessly backward in time. Instead, they'd subsist in time the way objects do in space. We could perpetually keep them as close as we'd like to ward off nostalgia. But we could also rush away from them as fast as we liked the instant they came to bore us.

On a final benign scenario the experiences of our lives would, by ramping up to a pace that approaches infinite speed, in effect cease moving backward in time. But in this case, they themselves would become the very units we would use to measure time. The more of them we compressed into our own mortal life, the longer—the closer to immortality—it would seem.

Unfortunately, each of these benign scenarios for immortality is outlandish. Each offers us endlessness reflected through a fun-house mirror. The self as a flowing liquid, dissolving in time. Experiences as solid objects, subsisting in time. The self expanding to encompass any measure of time. Experiences compressing and then becoming measures of time. If we have to rely on such convolutions to make immortality attractive, what does that say? And so I find them impossible finally to accept. They ask far too much of us: we who are recognizably human, who unavoidably see our selves as moving forward relentlessly in time—neither dissolving nor expanding in it—while the experiences of our lives flow remorselessly backward in time: neither subsisting nor compressing in it.[18]

For us, the only immortality scenarios on offer seem, sooner or later, utterly malignant. Each possible combination between our selves moving continually onward in time, and the events of our life moving ceaselessly backward in time, seems to carry storm clouds. Boredom if that onward-moving self and those backward-moving events at one point cease to change. Recurrent self-alienation if both self and events do endlessly change. Nostalgia if our self doesn't change, immured in old memories, attachments, and desires, while the events of our life ceaselessly do. And—although I won't explore this here—a kind of dementia if our self does continue to change, regularly jettisoning its previous memories and attachments and desires, while the events of our life no longer do. After all, when we try to think of people whose memories regularly empty out, who relinquish their previous emotional attachments, and whose desires wander erratically—but whose life events repeat themselves over and over—it's those afflicted with a kind of late-life dementia who come the closest.

But all of this is actually good news. It means we can be consoled by the thought that mortality has its blessings because immortality, for all we know now, would be a terrible curse. In Part Four, though, I consider one final matter: whether the losses we sustain due to death might actually be no worse than those we regularly suffer due to life itself anyway. "To lose . . . power, love, a friend—all are deaths," Michael Oakeshott writes, and "they are felt & suffered as deaths . . . these lesser deaths, the mortal material of our life—are the worst."[19] Perhaps life itself, with all its unpredictable ravages, sooner or later imposes each of the kinds of losses that death itself metes out. Life's losses intimate death's. If that's true, then that consoles us about death. The thought doesn't comfort us, perhaps, but it consoles us. Or so it's said.

But first, a brief interlude.

MORTALITY VERSUS IMMORTALITY:
WHY NOT THE RIGHT TO CHOOSE?

Some writers—the philosopher Jay Rosenberg, for example—have argued that the sharp dichotomy between mortality and immortality, as I have posed it throughout this book, is a false one. Preferable to either option would be a world in which we could, but did not have to, live forever. We would each enjoy life for as long as possible and then, if and when existence began to permanently pall, we would simply end it through some painless form of suicide.[1] We'd have a long life, maybe a hundreds-or-thousands-of-millennia-long life, depending on our preferences. And then whenever things started going sour, we'd bail out. The best of both worlds, life and death. Or, more exactly, a happy life, eons long, capped by a short end-period of unhappiness that would prompt us to terminate it before things got much worse. Clearly that would be preferable to either unavoidable mortality or compulsory immortality. Call this scenario "option immortality."

I wonder, however, whether option immortality, though perhaps preferable, is psychologically open to us. For us to be willing to terminate a happy life of great longevity, wouldn't it have to get so much worse at the end that it would outweigh all the good that came before? So that it would then no longer seem, in retrospect and on balance, to have been a happy life?

Look at it this way: It's true that as it is—mortals that we are—many of us reach a point where we wish to die due to the unhappy pain or debilities of advanced age. But we can still remain happy about the life we led because of the wonderful memories we have: because, as we recall it, it was a good life. Epicurus, for one, was in this circumstance. So why couldn't option-immortals do the same? Why couldn't they die remembering an extremely long happy life, which they then terminated as soon as it became painful or unpleasant?

The problem is that option-immortals, pondering whether to terminate their lives, would be in just the opposite situation. It wouldn't be one with happy memories that, as soon as unhappiness in the form of pain and debility irrevocably descended, they'd end. Instead, the immortal life I have been imagining throughout is one that, given scientific advances, is free of pain and debility. Unhappiness descends, if and when it does, precisely because the immortal's memories, happy though they once may have been, have begun to putrefy. Either the immortal's memories of the good times have disappeared altogether (self-alienation), or they have become crushingly stale (boredom), or they have become the very things that have prevented the immortal from adapting to unending novelty (nostalgia). For the option-immortal to be willing to die, wouldn't his entire previous life—as it exists in his memory—have to lose its value?

Or look at it this way: option-immortals, presumably, wouldn't terminate their life simply if things got a little worse. After all, the longer a life is or can be, the more serious and weighty a proposition it is to consider ending it. That's why the centenarians in Shaw's *Back to Methuselah* are so much more accident-averse than we decadarians are.[2] Instead, things would have to get a whole lot worse. Option-immortals would bring themselves to terminate a life of vastly heightened longevity only when things got so much worse that, looking back, they would no longer, on balance, see the value of their life at all—only when, on balance, they would rather not have lived at all. Or at least I wonder if that's not the risk. The best of both worlds, life and death, won't necessarily be possible if immortality is an option. For option-immortals to be willing to choose death, they would have to have lost contact with their life in some profound way.

And so in examining consolations for mortality, I have taken mortality's alternative to be not optional but irreversible immortality. I am skeptical of the idea of a comforting middle ground, namely longevity for as long as life is happy, and then, as soon as it becomes unhappy, painless suicide. Though logically possible, I'm not sure how psychologically realistic that trick would be. It would require us to feel enough unhappiness to want to die while still remaining happy about the life we led.

Many have criticized Epicurus for assuming that human beings could ever become sufficiently unattached to life that we would be indifferent to and accepting of death, yet still sufficiently attached to life that we wouldn't actually kill ourselves. The same kind of fine, perhaps impossible, balance would be required for a long-lived human to—at one and the same time—continue to view the life he led as a happy one, while having become sufficiently unhappy that he would be willing to end it. If he views his life as happy, he will not want to end it. And if he wants to end it, because the depredations of immortality have sufficiently set in, will he any longer be able to view it as having been a happy one? I don't know, of course, but there is reason to think not. Option-immortality, like an option in the stock market, is far from a sure bet.

PART 4

Life Intimates Death

thirteen

THE BIG SLEEP

Death has rarely appeared as beguiling as it does in Lampedusa's novel *The Leopard*, toward the book's end. It is impossible to completely convey the allure of Lampedusa's imagery because its full punch comes from a sly bit of foreshadowing. But, toward the end, death takes the form of a young woman, lovely, modest, desirous. Gently nudging the dying old prince's gathered and sobbing relatives out of the way, she finally arrives at his bedside. Until that moment, the delirium in the prince's mind had seemed to him like a thunderous ocean. And then, when the woman at last is beside him, the "crashing of the sea subside[s] altogether."[1]

In the gallery of sensory images for death, silence has one great competitor: darkness. For Lampedusa, death might be the subsiding of the roaring of the sea. But for Harold Brodkey, it is "this wild darkness." For Andrew Marvell, the grave is a "fine and quiet place." For Dylan Thomas, death is famously a "dying of the light" to be raged against. None of this surprises, since silence and darkness constitute the conditions most conducive to sleep. And so when we imagine the "big sleep," we imagine eternal silence, eternal darkness.

Death portends a horrific loss, the loss of consciousness itself. But we lose consciousness in life all the time. Does the silence and darkness of dreamless sleep intimate death? And if so, is that a consolatory thought?

Yet as they pile up, a difference between aural and visual images of death, between silence and darkness, slowly emerges. As silence, death can seem attractive—calm, tranquil, peaceful, restful. As darkness, it comes across as menacing—cold, desolate, bereft, bleak. Darkness itself is so unappealing that even when it's accompanied by the opposite of silence—by sounds—the result can seem hellish: think of a pitch-dark ghoulishly acousticed horror ride in an amusement park.

Silence, by contrast, can be so beckoning that as soon as it's joined to the opposite of darkness—joined to light—the result can rise to the rapturous: think of the silence of a sunlit meadow.[2]

Why does darkness threaten more than silence? Perhaps an investigation of ordinary language can help here. The aural word "sound" has not one but two visual equivalents: "sight"—as in "sights and sounds"—and "light," as in "sound and light show." That's because any given object of sight—a ball, a book—and the light source that allows us to see it—the sun, a lamp—are usually distinct entities. By contrast, the source of a sound and the object we hear as a result—think of a racing car or an overflying plane—are one and the same. All you have to do is shut off the light, and even with innumerable sight-making objects present you won't see them. But to shut off sound, you must get rid of or tamper with each sound-making object.

In *Heart of Darkness* Conrad contrasts the darkness with the whiteness that Marlow encounters in Africa. Darkness is horror. Whiteness, especially the whiteness of the river fog, is confusion. In other words, what Conrad does *not* do is contrast Africa's darkness with its more natural opposite—lightness—because that would imply that European civilization is somehow more enlightened. Nor does he contrast whiteness with its natural opposite, blackness, which would have given his work a far more racialist tone than it already has. Instead, it's darkness versus whiteness. Conrad is able to do this because the visual world offered him two scales to play with, black/white for the objects of sight; darkness/light for the source of illumination that reveals them.

And therein lies the key to why darkness, absence of light, will always be more bereft and desolate than silence, absence of sound. In darkness, the source of light to all objects is cut off. Sight is impossible; it is hopeless. In silence, by contrast, all that we know is that no particular object surrounding us is at the moment a source of sound. But at any other moment it or others still could be—there is no blanket source that has been extinguished, and so silence comes with hope. If we say that it's so quiet you could hear a pin drop, we hold out the possibility that you could still—despite the silence—hear a pin drop. But we could never say that it's so dark you could see a pin drop. There'd be no hope of that.

We have reason, then, to feel peaceful and secure when we think of death in Hamlet's terms—the deep rest that is silence—while when we think of it in William Styron's phrase—lie down in darkness—we feel cold and afraid. True, both metaphors fall squarely into the class of magical thinking. When we are dead we will experience neither silence nor darkness. But silence and darkness are as close as we can get, this side of death, to intimations of what lies on the other side. They are the metaphors of choice for great writers who find themselves consoled by silence and desolated by darkness. But in the final analysis the only reason why silence is less threatening is that it's more fragile than darkness. Any sound can end it, and make the world alive again, while no sight alone can end darkness. It's not that death seems more attractive when we think of it as silence. It's actually that silence is more attractive because it is less like death.

So despite the great literature they have inspired, our different reactions to darkness and silence ultimately say nothing about death itself—only about us and the way we sense, and cling to, the living world. If true intimations of death in life are what we seek, we shall have to look elsewhere. And apart from the darkness and silence we associate with sleep, life offers us one other kind of intimation of the utter sensory void that comes after our death: it's the inkling we have of the utter sensory void that came before our birth.[3]

The Rocking Cradle

"The cradle rocks above an abyss," Nabokov says, "and common sense tells us that our existence is but a brief crack of light between two eternities of darkness."

Perhaps that is common sense. But then Nabokov says something more controversial. He describes those two dark eternities as "identical twins." And in so doing, he gestures toward a famous query Lucretius posed thousands of years before. We remain undisturbed by the eternity of darkness that elapsed prior to our birth. Why, then—since the two are carbon copies—be petrified about the eternity of darkness to follow our deaths?

Yes, in a sense the two are carbon copies. We don't exist during either of them. But what's of interest here is not Nabokov's take on those two boundless spans of dark time. It's the imagery he uses for the compressed mortal life that separates them. He calls it a tiny "crack" of light. That's a spatial image. In the picture Nabokov paints, it's not a brief temporal interlude but a minuscule crack of space that separates the two dark eternities in time.

But how can a span of space separate two periods in time? Space is static. It doesn't flow in the way time does. As an image for our abbreviated interval of existence, a crack of space utterly fails to represent life's remorseless temporal current: the current that sweeps every one of us, second by second, beginning with the instant of our birth and ending at the moment of our death, further and further away from the dark eternity lying behind and closer and closer to the dark eternity lying ahead.

Yes, those two dark eternities, the prenatal and the posthumous, might well be identical as far as we would be concerned during their endless eons. But it's as if Nabokov knew that anything that's consolatory about that observation would immediately fall away were we to consider the relentless one-directional flow of the brief time that separates them: the flow that makes the prenatal dark eternity seem anodyne and the posthumous one spell annihilation. Only when we obscure that temporal flow with static spatial imagery, and describe our life as (say) a tiny crack, will the two dark eternities on either side stand a chance of seeming "identical." In space, unlike in time, nothing would necessarily be carrying us ceaselessly away from the one and toward the other. We could be neutral between them.

Perhaps Nabokov's imagery is no coincidence. Two millennia earlier Lucretius, in advancing his famous consolation—we're indifferent to the eternal darkness lying behind us, so why shouldn't we be just as unperturbed by the one lying ahead?—did something similar.

In the verses commonly called *Folly of the Fear of Death*, Lucretius speaks of the periods before birth and after death as "times [of] slumber . . . sleep and rest." And in between the two, where the "light of life shines," we human beings get put, Lucretius says, in "place." Interesting. In Lucretius's rendering, it seems to be a place of light—as for Nabokov it's a crack of light—that separates the dark times before and after.

Elsewhere Lucretius equates life to a room, or to a banquet hall. He also says that none of us own our lives outright. Instead we merely lease them, as if life were a tract of land instead of a river of time. Perhaps Lucretius knew that only by suggestively wrapping our temporally flowing life in inanimate spatial symbols—like place and land and room and hall—could he even come close to portraying the two slumber times on either side as equivalent.

What about we who inhabit the illuminated space that Lucretius equates with life? What are human selves like? Lucretius uses analogies—and curiously static ones at that—to describe us. Anguished and unrequited lovers, he says, mimic "Tityus prostrate": prostrate while vultures munch on his liver. Those of us who fear the torments of Hell remind Lucretius of "Tantalus benumbed": benumbed by the giant rock hanging over his head. And weary, defeated politicians channel Sisyphus, eternally pushing his rock up the mountain only to have it tumble down such that he must start over: Sisyphus, who, far from marching forward linearly, just keeps cycling in position.

But these mythical figures—never moving in space—scarcely represent us mortal creatures, ever moving in time, ferried unrelentingly further and further away from the eternal slumber in back and nearer and nearer to the one in front. Nabokov's rocking cradle doesn't move forward either, just back and forth like Sisyphus.[4]

A more apt image comes from Schopenhauer. "A man," Schopenhauer says, "finds himself, to his great astonishment, suddenly existing, after thousands and thousands of years of non-existence: he lives for a little while; and then, again, comes an equally long period when he must exist no more." During that "little while" of life—and a "while," of course, is a stretch of time, not a stretch of space—do we remain inert and inanimate? Not for Schopenhauer. No, we resemble "a man running downhill, who cannot keep on his legs unless he runs on, and will inevitably fall if he stops."[5] That's more like it. Not statically suspended between two identical dark eternities, but running as fast as he can—because he is compelled to do so—away from the one shrinking harmlessly in view behind him, and toward the one growing ever more menacingly larger ahead.

That's how we twenty-first century bundles of ego and anxiety see our selves too. And so the eternal darkness before we were born, as we think of it from within the confines of our abbreviated mortal life, can never intimate the one to come. By depicting life as a kind of stationary place, and our selves who inhabit it as immobile, Lucretius subtly drapes our mortal existence in a timeless spatial imagery that casts the two dark eternities on either side as interchangeable twins. But such a gambit simply gives away how psychologically unpersuasive his argument really is. He could never have made the same case while picturing our selves and our lives as they actually are: our selves moving ceaselessly forward in time, our lives relentlessly propelling us—second by second—away from the one dark eternity and toward the other. In the end, Lucretius's consolation, on which eternal posthumous darkness should leave us as serene as eternal prenatal darkness, will gain purchase with hardly any of us.

When we die, Philip Roth proclaims, we "enter . . . into nowhere without even knowing it."[1] Or as that other Philip, Larkin, puts it— and it is his words that now claim a kind of patent on this bleak point—consolations for death amount to

> specious stuff that says No rational being
> Can fear a thing it will not feel, not seeing
> That this is what we fear—no sight, no sound,
> No touch or taste or smell, nothing to think with,
> Nothing to love or link with,
> The anasthetic from which none come round.[2]

Specious stuff: it's all very well to claim that death is benign. Or that if we reflect on it, we will see that anything we might seek from an immortal life we can actually attain within the confines of our mortal existence. Or that real immortality would actually be terrible. But none of this philosophizing addresses the raw loss that death imposes: the loss of that precious flicker, the light of consciousness. Console me about that, Larkin challenges. His poetry lends poignant beauty to the primal bark of raw emotion. After all the reasoning and all the rationales, I'd still desperately prefer to be a conscious, healthy human being than a corpse. Who wouldn't?

But suppose that's not the choice we face.

Consider two contemporary opponents in the debate over whether mortality is a good thing, Leon Kass and Ray Kurzweil. Kass, a physician and philosopher, prefers death to immortality. But he goes one step further. He sees death as a grace-bestowed relief from life itself when that life, the life of the human organism, begins to degrade into indignity and debility. As the process of organic deterioration that commences well before we die—first sans teeth, then sans eyes, then sans taste—painfully progresses, the prospect of death becomes more and more welcome. And what is death but the continuation of that organismic breakdown—first sans flesh and then sans bones—as we crumble into dust "a-blowing down the night," returning to the soil, the air, and the sea.

Kurzweil, the scientist and visionary, prefers immortality to death. But he too goes one step further. He favors immortality over human life itself, looking forward as he does to the day when the life of the human species becomes outmoded and we all merge into a collective, higher-order, eternal cosmic consciousness. We will be driven to do so by the so-called singularity—the inevitable moment when computers become more intelligent than humans, encouraging us for the sake of survival to "upload" our own individual minds into a mass silicon-based superintelligence. No longer chained to the dying animal that comprises our carbon-based bodies, we will share both omniscience and immortality.

I note that Kurzweil, along with Hans Moravec, Marvin Minsky, and other like-minded visionaries, finds it exceedingly difficult to describe exactly what this metamorphosis would be like. Moravec, for example, speaks of us humans embarking on a "subtle cyberspace conversion, the whole becoming finally a bubble of Mind expanding at near lightspeed."[3] As the author Vernor Vinge observes in Churchillian tones, "an opaque wall [has descended] across the future."[4] But despite the fog that lies ahead, all of them—Vinge and the others—seem certain that humanity is heading in that posthuman direction.

It was Kurzweil who, in 1990, foresaw that a computer would beat a world champion at chess. And in 1997 it happened when IBM's supercomputer, known as "Deep Blue," defeated Garry Kasparov. Perhaps, then, Kurzweil is thinking of our all merging into some gigantic version of Deep Blue.[5] Let's take that as the closest proxy for what he and the others have in mind.

Both of these human futures—our blending into a universal mind and our crumbling into the physical universe—share a common feature. Together, they reframe the ultimate choice we think we have, inviting us to view it in a different way. Not, as we typically do, as a choice between our remaining forever conscious and our becoming permanently unconscious. Instead, it's a choice between our becoming *part* of a larger immortal consciousness—a single all-embracing superintelligence, an omniscient Deep Blue—or becoming *part* of a larger permanent unconsciousness: the cosmos of rocks, dust, molecules, atoms. When the singularity arrives it will force each of us to make a decision. We could either upload our consciousnesses into the universal mind, or we could remain "original substrate" humans, biological humans who—as they always have done—will die, dissolve into particles, and "drop back," in Willa Cather's words, "into the immense design of things": the physical universe.

Let's entertain the possibility that this is how we should look at the choice toward which destiny is taking us: merge into the universal mind or dissolve into the physical universe. Something like these two options, many smart people are telling us, will be our fate sooner or later. What, then, would be the better alternative? Those smart people have no doubt: become part of the cosmic consciousness. Are they right? Or would it be better to become part of the cosmos itself?

There once was an amiable and capable Canadian cabinet minister named Harvie Andre. One evening Andre dropped in on a party at the opulent home of an Ottawa lobbyist, a man who had been conducting a lucrative business representing clients to Andre and his office. Surveying the expanse of elegance and exquisiteness that lay all around him, Andre famously quipped, "Why is it so much better to know Harvie Andre than to be Harvie Andre?"

Would it be better to become part of the cosmic consciousness that comes to know the beauty and secrets of the cosmos—secrets that remain totally beyond our current ken—or to become part of that mysterious, fascinating cosmos itself?

I understand what it means to become part of the cosmos. It means that my body will return to organic nature, dissolving over time into molecules—compressed into a rock, osmotically engorged by a tree, food for snails, a home for fleas, a nest for birds, atoms in a galactic storm, or back to where it all began, the sea, each particle lasting forever. What does it mean, though, to become part of cosmic consciousness, the posthuman collective consciousness that spends eternity knowing the cosmos? It's hard to get a grip on that.

And for good reason. Consciousness, unlike the cosmos, is unitary. There is no such thing as being a "part" of a larger cosmic consciousness in the way one can become part of—particles in—the larger cosmos.

To say that consciousness is unitary doesn't imply that consciousness *is* just one thing, as opposed to a grab bag of different functions—visual, aural, cognitive, and the like. It simply means, as John Searle says, that we always have a "unified conscious field. At any moment you do not just experience the sound of the music and the taste of the beer, but you have both as part of a single, unified conscious field, a subjective awareness of the total conscious experience."[6] Certainly, the kind of hyperaware cosmic consciousness of which Kurzweil speaks, one that has no secrets from itself—one with nothing even hidden in the basement of an unconscious[7]—would be unitary in this way. And so "we" would have been obliterated. To use the words that Kurzweil himself favors, we would "meld" and "merge" into the unitary whole of cosmic consciousness, not remain discrete entities within it.[8]

True, not all versions of cosmic consciousness envision our merging and melding. N. Katherine Hayles, a perceptive critic of the Kurzweil-type vision, speaks of what she calls a "distributed" universal consciousness. We would each play our own separate part in a glorified version of—to use the psychologist Daniel Wegner's analogy—the "group mind" of a typical household. As Wegner, in a *New York Times* article, recounted his domestic scene, "I remembered where the car and yard things were, she [Wegner's wife] remembered where the house things were, and we could each depend on the other to be an expert in domains we didn't need to master."[9] Because he and his spouse remained distinct individuals within their household cybermind, Wegner foresaw that the same could be true in the universal cybermind. That's why his article is called "Don't Fear the Cybermind," and why he spoke of our one day each becoming "*part* of the biggest, smartest mind ever." In Wegner's vision, then, individual consciousness would remain; the parts wouldn't dissolve into the whole.

But that's because there would be no real universal mind. No entity in "distributed" cosmic consciousness would, actually, possess cosmic consciousness, knowing where both the yard and the household things are. By contrast, in true "cosmic consciousness," as William James long ago realized, it's impossible to imagine what "individuation" would look like.[10]

While true cosmic consciousness might obliterate individuality, and while distributed consciousness might preserve individuality at the cost of not being truly cosmic, visionaries like Ray Kurzweil himself seem to toggle, unresolved, between the two possibilities. Kurzweil certainly heralds the moment when we will all meld and merge into a true cosmic mind. But according to Benjamin Mitchell-Yellin, the philosopher who helped run the Templeton Foundation's Immortality Project, Kurzweil also "doesn't like the single global consciousness idea, because he thinks that it would preclude him being there. He assumes that his individual self would not persist."[11]

Kurzweil seems conflicted. Indeed, at one point in his book *The Age of Spiritual Machines*, Kurzweil gestures toward this dilemma but without ever grasping its horns. He inquires of an imagined superhuman collective intelligence: "So, you separate your personalities . . ." and the entity responds, "At times. But we still share our knowledge stores at all times."[12] Kurzweil, then, evidently sees some kind of trade-off between shared knowledge and the separation of personalities, between true cosmic consciousness and individual survival. But he offers no indication of how they might be reconciled. Perhaps that's because they can't be.

So let's suppose, as many a visionary predicts—whether he or she welcomes or fears it—that the choice that one day will confront us is to either dissolve into true cosmic consciousness or else become particles in the cosmos itself. Either future "humans" would at one point after birth get uploaded, losing their individuality in the universal mind—or else they would remain individual biological organisms, living and dying in the time-honored way, before crumbling into the physical universe. What's the better option?

True, this is a deliberately polarizing choice. There may in fact lie innumerable shades of gray in between. Human beings could easily retain their individuality without remaining entirely biological organisms. They might one day integrate complex computational hardware into their individual organic brains, and in so doing they might each attain ever greater individual intelligence short of cosmic consciousness. But my purpose here is not to speculate about possible futures, or about the vast range of scenarios scientists have floated for our acquiring ever more powerful individual minds situated on vastly extended silicon-based substrates. Instead, it's to look at whether there's anything consolatory to be gleaned from thinking about the stark choice between our merging into a vastly extended cosmic mind and our clinging, instead, to our individual, doomed-to-crumble, carbon-based physical substrates.

In the end, I think it's better to be Harvie Andre than to know Harvie Andre. It's better to crumble into the physical cosmos than merge into a cosmic consciousness that spends eons contemplating that cosmos. Why? Because it's better to be an object of admiration than the one doing the admiring.

True, it's better to be a *conscious* admirer, like an art connoisseur, than an *unconscious* object of admiration, like a work of art. But if both are on the same level—if both admirer and admired are conscious (think of Jimmy Stewart and Katharine Hepburn in *The Philadelphia Story*), then it's better to be the "object" being admired. And so if instead "you" will be *un*conscious either way, why not be part of the object being admired rather than dissolve into the subject doing the admiring?

Emotionally, I find myself gravitating toward the imagery writers use to describe our becoming particles in the cosmos itself—the molecules of my body becoming flowers and trees, sustenance for worms, motes in the sunlight that warms the earth, stardust, a comet's tail, diffused into the mother of life, the sea. It's a process that begins well before we die, as the Canadian actress Linda Griffiths so acidly noted in her play *Maggie and Pierre*, in which the twenty-two-year-old Margaret Trudeau describes brushing her lips against those of the fifty-two-year-old Pierre as akin to kissing a drying rose petal.[13] In contrast to these organic metaphors, the lifeless pictures conjured up to give us some sense of what cosmic consciousness would be like—melding into a matrix or a hologram, merging into a code or an algorithm—leave me metallically cold.

As part of the cosmos, I might disintegrate into billions of particles, into what Edna St. Vincent Millay calls "dull . . . indiscriminate dust." But that dust will go "to feed the roses," the poet says, and "fragrant is the blossom." My "bone ash" will rise "in the saplings . . . passing into the shells of snails, the bones of fish and birds."[14] It will go back to a kind of life, a part of Gaia, the organic respiration of the planet. But meld into cosmic consciousness? That's not life but death. The singularity prognosticator Ben Goertzel unwittingly makes the point: "If it came down to it, I wouldn't hesitate to annihilate myself in favor of some amazing superbeing."[15] What's key here is the equation of merger into a superconsciousness with annihilation.

But of course this is all a kind of magical thinking. It's impossible for an individual to experience either dissolving into cosmic consciousness or becoming particulate matter in the cosmos itself. And yet like much magical thinking, this instance too clues us into a deeper psychological reality. At some level we rightly fear that although we will not be physically obliterated in the cosmos itself— our particles will last forever—we would be mentally obliterated in cosmic consciousness. No parts of us would remain.

Perhaps a better way of putting it would be to say that in the future as imagined by Kurzweil and company, either "option"—cosmic consciousness or the cosmos itself—would spell death and the dreaded annihilation it entails for individual consciousness. It's just that it would be the death of the individual in the case of our melding into cosmic consciousness. And it would be the death of consciousness in the case of our particles blending into the cosmos itself. We would thus lose individual consciousness whether we lived or died. And so life, if we opted for Kurzweil's cosmic consciousness, truly would intimate death—even when it comes to the most fearful loss that death can deal, the loss of individual consciousness. If that's our future, then perhaps we do abide in the best of times, a beautiful bubble in history, right now, before we have to face the choice between *individual* consciousness and individual *consciousness*. And maybe that's some consolation.

It's funny. The question on the table is whether the losses that life deals us are, when it comes right down to it, any different from those that death imposes. If no difference emerges, then we should feel at least weakly consoled about our mortality.

But my "priors," before examining the question, would have led me to believe that while the mere vicissitudes of life can take from us many of the same things that our death ultimately does—a spouse (if her affections wander), children (if their anger estranges them), businesses, jobs, homes, homelands—the one loss that life can never deal us is the loss of individual consciousness. The ebbs and flows of life can take from us many, perhaps all, of the beloved objects that populate our consciousness, I would have thought—and especially our lovers, friends, sons, and daughters—with every bit as much finality as our own death does. But life can never, I would have thought, destroy our own bare individual subject itself the way that death can.

It's actually more the reverse. The one death-dealt loss that life too can inflict, at least potentially, turns out to be the loss of subjective individual consciousness. Human life, if the cosmic-consciousness visionaries are right in their prognoses, will finally terminate individual consciousness, even if (perversely) so many of them seem to welcome that prospect. Meanwhile, all those other losses—the losses of all the objects of our consciousness, and in particular the people we moon over and obsess over and spin over and over in our minds? It turns out, as I will argue in the next chapter, that the tragedies—the conflicts and failures, however devastating—of human relationships, of life itself, can never deprive us of those we love in the way that our death does. And that, too, is a good thing. While it doesn't console me about death, it consoles me about life. And I need that too.

Of course, my own individual consciousness is what I want most of all. I'd rather be a cognizant, sentient human being than a corpse. But if the day ever comes, I'd turn down the chance to dissolve into computational consciousness, into the universal mind. Instead I'd choose to become a lasting part of living, organic nature, part of the physical universe.

Meld into Deep Blue? No thanks. I'd rather merge into the deep blue sea.

fifteen

EVERY TIME I SAY GOODBYE, I DIE A LITTLE

"For forty years I saw myself through John's eyes," Joan Didion writes in *The Year of Magical Thinking*; "I did not age."[1]

It's an affecting thought. A husband looks at his sixty-nine-year-old wife and habitually, reflexively, sees the twenty-nine-year-old he first knew. His doing so is contagious. She too comes to view herself in the same way. Only when the husband then dies does the wife—for "the first year since I was twenty-nine," as Didion says—suddenly see "that my image of myself was of someone significantly younger."

An affecting thought, but also a paradoxical one. For consider the main theme of Didion's book: her lingering sense, over the course of the subsequent year, that John was not dead but on an out-of-town trip. At any moment he would "return and need his shoes" or jackets or chair or office. Certainly that's what the evidence suggested. The planet continued to bear his physical imprint as clearly as ever. He might have been gone but the world retained—in exactly the way it always had whenever he was simply somewhere else—the spaces, whether small ones like sneakers or large ones like dens, that he would come home to occupy.

Put the two together: on the one hand, when John was alive, he kept Joan frozen in time, ageless as a young woman. On the other hand, once John died, Joan kept him moving forward in time, persisting as a breathing, organic creature. The living Joan never moved beyond twenty-nine; John, dead at seventy-one, continued to live on. Each thought bookends the other.

Whatever you might think of the other consolatory streams—that death for one reason or another is actually benign, that mortality gives us all we could ever gain from immortality, or that immortality for one reason or another would actually be gruesome—you might still not be able to get past death's most massive affront: the devastating and overwhelming losses it inflicts, the final farewells it forces us to bid to everyone and everything we love. I am here interested in the loss not of consciousness itself, as I was in the last chapter, but of all the things in the world that attract and delight our consciousness: the loss not of the subject of consciousness but of all its objects. And yet what if all of the losses that we would sustain in death, all its poignant permanent goodbyes, can and would come with life anyway? Shouldn't that, at least in a backhanded way, console us about our mortality?

Many have thought so. Since our "world is a world of continuous loss," the psychiatrist Adam Phillips argues, "all the quotidian experiences of loss, all the disappearances of everyday life, are like rehearsals" for "the hidden drama of one's own death."[2] Yes, death might bring tremendous "loss," the poet Kate Clanchy acknowledges, "but, in a way, I had lost plenty of friends just through life's ordinary processes—they had moved away or married someone I didn't like."[3] Or consider John Updike, in a story whose main character encounters a former lover: "I felt in her presence the fear of death a man feels with a woman who once opened herself to him and is available no more."[4]

So the idea on the table for consideration—the putatively consoling idea—is that all the losses that death brings would come with life anyway: and I am, as I have been throughout, setting aside losses due to physical decline and decrepitude. Let's focus, then, on the sharpest kind of losses that your death will bring: the heart-clutching thought that the hour will arrive when you must part for eternity from everyone you love—soul mate, lover, children, friends. Never more, as Lucretius says, "will your happy home give you welcome"; never more "will your [spouse] and sweet children race to win the first kisses, and thrill your heart to its depths with sweetness." Now: in what way does life itself impose similar losses, force equivalent goodbyes?

Think of the countless opportunities we all lose in life as precious moments vanish forever into the past. Weren't we, for example, unavoidably stuck in Philadelphia on business the night our daughter played the role of Anita in the grade-six production of *West Side Story* at her Toronto middle school? Well then, in what sense would it matter, would it be any more a loss, if we missed our great-great-grandson's performance as Officer Krupke because we were dead? What difference is there between a loss due to your being out of town and a loss due to your no longer being on the surface of the earth? You lose the same thing in either case. No difference might be apparent even to the one with whom you lost the opportunity to spend time. It seemed to Didion not that Dunne had died, but that he had simply gone somewhere else—annoyingly out of town, in Los Angeles, say, when she, remaining in their New York apartment surrounded by his chair and desk and shoes, needed to ask his advice on a literary or household matter. In Jim Crace's novel *Being Dead*, a daughter imagines her departed father reassuring her with a similar thought: "Death is nothing at all. I have slipped away into another room. All is well."[5]

But if we can so easily analogize death to an unavoidable business trip when our daughter performed on stage, or an unfortunate slipping away to the bathroom just when our infant son took his first step, then is there really any difference between what we lose when we die and what we necessarily lose countless times while alive? Simply add up all the past moments when we couldn't be with our children because they had to be in school—when the joke they made broke the class up, say, or they made a priceless remark to the teacher or showed the first blossoming of moral courage in taking an unpopular stance—and we had to be at the office. In life itself, we miss precious moment after precious moment, surrendering them forever because we cannot be in all places at the same time. And so why rip our hearts out over all the future moments we lose because, thanks to death, we can't be in the same place with our children for all time? As the philosopher Charles Hartshorne once put it: "To be finite or limited in time is no more an injury than to be finite in space."[6]

So lost moments are continually slipping into the past, second by second, gone forever. Meanwhile, we ourselves and those we love continually forge ahead, year by year, into the future. But then isn't it inevitable that, sooner or later, life itself will part us and we will irrecoverably lose one another? Are we not, after all, kidding ourselves if we think that our sweet children, once they blossom and mature, will always want to stay with us—or even have anything to do with us?

People grow apart. Someone who exists for thousands of years cannot expect his grandchildren to still be calling him every week, as Mel Brooks's two-thousand-year-old man ruefully observed, or even every millennium. Live long enough (and long enough might not be all that long) and we will all become Lears abandoned by Regans. Or Helmers by Noras. Even in our current mortal life spans, as Didion says, "Husbands walk out, wives walk out." When Rosemary Clooney began singing "We'll Be Together Again," she "was imagining the end of a love affair; she later sang it thinking of the friends who've died too young"[7]—just as if the two kinds of losses, the one due to the ebbing of love during life and the other to the finality of death, were cut from the same cloth. But let Shelley's celebrated words make the point:

> All things that we love and cherish,
> Like ourselves must fade and perish;
> Such is our rude mortal lot—
> Love itself would, did they not.

If we didn't lose others due to death, we'd lose them due to life. What's the difference?

So we have on the table the consoling (if hardly cheering) thought that the most devastating losses we sustain in death, its excruciating ultimate goodbyes, would come with life anyway. Even while we are alive, we lose countless moments with loved ones, moments that disappear irretrievably into the past. And we will or would eventually lose those loved ones themselves when, as our respective selves move ever forward into the future, we grow ever increasingly distant. The consoling thought, then, is that the losses that life brings, at least for those of us who value human relationships above everything else— for we people who need people—are ultimately no different than those that death inflicts.

Does this consolation for mortality ring true?

Suppose that you missed your son's performance in Toronto, although you were able to close the biggest merger deal of your life, because you were in Philadelphia that same evening. Is this any different from missing his musical performance in 2020, although you were able to close the biggest merger deal of your life in 2018, because you died in 2019? Life itself necessitates your being finite in space. Death simply returns the compliment by necessitating that you're finite in time. What's the difference?

It's simply this: Life itself might make it impossible for you to be in two different places at the same time. But it doesn't prevent you from being in the same place with your son at a different time. You might have missed his performance in Toronto because you had to be in Philadelphia that evening. But you can still be with him when he graduates later that year. As the old Harry Chapin song has it, "We'll get together then, son." But suppose you missed his performance in 2020 because you died in 2019. Then you can never make up for it.

If we didn't die, then we'd eliminate a kind of loss that goes over and above anything that life itself imposes. In this sense, life's losses do not and cannot intimate death's.

What about the observation that even if we somehow never lost opportunities to be with our loved ones, we would sooner or later grow ever more distant from them, and so lose them that way? Wouldn't life's losses then ultimately match death's?

But again, "distant" is a spatial concept. While two people can move apart in space, whether due to estrangement or for some other reason, they cannot move apart in time. Your fed-up spouse can leave you behind in Toledo by moving to Pittsburgh. But she cannot leave you behind in 2016 by moving to 2017 or 2117. While the two of you might no longer occupy the same spatial location for the rest of your lives, you will still always occupy precisely the same moment in time, millisecond by millisecond—until one of you dies. In *Mrs. Dalloway*, the critic Victor Brombert notes, "Big Ben can be heard throughout, solemn and majestic, marking the irrevocable hour, accompanying Clarissa and Peter Walsh on their separate walks through the city, providing a sense of simultaneity and a link between one isolated consciousness and another."[8]

As long as we live—we and our lovers, spouses, or children who have deserted us for different far-flung places in space—we will always remain enveloped in the same moment in time, the same temporal environment, the same events of the world, events of the culture, events of the family, all of which provide innumerable possible points of psychological closeness. Crooning "Are you lonesome tonight?" Elvis wonders whether his absent lover misses his presence in her home, her living room, her porch. Life's losses, Elvis tells us, are spatial. We grew apart, and what remains is an empty chair and a bare doorstep. Life's losses, though, are not temporal. The question "Are you lonesome tonight?" assumes that Elvis and his lover still share the exact same "tonight," the exact same moment and always will—until one of them dies. For as long as they live they can never escape one another in time.

So yes, life itself makes it all too possible for you and your lover to be in two disparate places at the same time; life itself can and does separate us in space. But nothing about life makes it possible for you and she to be at two different moments in time, she stopping in 2019 while you move on to 2020. Only death can force that kind of parting. In that sense, too, life's losses can never intimate death's.

Statues and Trophies

At first glance, it would seem as if we can make short work of the idea that life's losses resemble death's. Yes, husbands walk out, wives walk out, and there have been countless moments when we were separated from our sweet children. But those losses will never rival the ones that death imposes. As long as we live, we will always be at the same moment in time as our wayward spouse even if at a different place. And as long as we live, we can always be at the same place with our sweet children at other moments.

But let's press this a little further. Who really thinks that even if we always occupy the same moment with our wayward spouse as we move forward in time together, that that has any meaning at all if we can't also be in the same place? And sure, we can always be at the same place with our child at a later moment. But who really thinks that our doing so would compensate for the irreplaceable loss of missing his first step or his recital or any number of other precious moments, watching them slide irrecoverably into the past? "How many fathers haven't been around for their children's birthdays, or their first step, because they were working," Spike Lee ruminates, or "OK . . . at a Knicks game. And when you miss it, it's gone. That's a lot of guilt."[9]

What precisely, then, is so wonderful about our mortal condition—in which we all move forward together second by second in time while the moments of our lives slip ceaselessly through our fingers back into the past? It seems quite compatible with heaping helpings of loss, even if they don't exactly resemble death's.

But actually, there is something wonderful about our condition.

Let's think, for a moment, about what the world would be like if we weren't all compelled to move forward together, second by second, in time. On first glance, it might seem to have its attractive features. Wouldn't it be nice if instead of marching into the future moment by moment in lockstep, temporally manacled to all our fellow existing human beings—Elvis to his lover, Clarissa to Peter—we could somehow move freely in time just as we can in space? Wouldn't it be terrific if you could continue forging ahead in time if you wanted to, while I could hang back for a bit—or indefinitely—at my favorite age or year, if that suited me? We enjoy such freedom of movement in space. Why not in time?

Think of how we imagine people who cease moving ahead in time while others continue on. We can't seem to do it without envisaging those who choose to stop moving—who opt to get off of time's conveyor belt—as statues. Recall those TV commercials showing a busy executive moving briskly toward her rental car while everyone around her, having foolishly chosen to rent from a competitor, is paralyzed. Or the nonaging hero in Charles Maturin's *Melmoth the Wanderer*, who's described as a "statue," his hand "as cold as that of death."[10] Or what about Dorian Gray, who ceases to age while his picture, along with everyone else, continues to grow older? Dorian "never carved a statue," his frenemy Harry says, "or painted a picture . . ." Instead, Dorian himself is a statue, or a picture, having stopped moving forward in time.

A statue is not—nor is it meant to be—an attractive image for the self. No, it is a cautionary conceit designed to ward us off of thinking that anything other than our common, inescapable movement forward in time is desirable. Note that Dorian never *literally* stops moving forward in time while others continue on. That would require some fancy metaphysics. Rather, he stops in some ways but not in others. He stops physically aging, even as he continues to accumulate more experiences and memories as the years pass. That physical stasis, however—and this is the point—is enough to open up a complete rupture between him and his fellow human beings. It's enough to wrench him out of the common experience of humankind. It creates an ever-widening gulf between him and all others, who do continue to move ahead in time and grow old. Dorian loses them, and he in turn becomes lost to them. He becomes dead to them. Like a statue.

And that makes sense. After all, in our human experience thus far, there's only one way in which two people can part in time, one continuing to move ahead and the other ceasing to do so. It's if the second one dies. Had we the freedom to move—or not—in time the way we do in space, we would simply take a form of loss that only death can inflict and make it a part of life.

In fact, we have seen this idea before—the idea of a self ceasing to move forward in time if it so chooses—in Chapter 1. No one, as the philosopher J. David Velleman points out, thinks of a statue as traveling inch by inch through space from its feet toward the top of its head. In like fashion, we needn't view our selves as traveling moment by moment through time from our births toward our deaths. Instead, just as no part of a statue—and of course a part is all that exists at any given point in space—can be said to be moving toward the ceiling, no part of our self—and, after all, a part is all that ever exists at any given moment in time—can be said to be moving toward our death.

Suppose we adopt this mindset. Just as a statue's nose grows no taller than its knee, the 10–11 AM, August 8, 2020, part of our self—as we see it—will grow no older than the 10–11 AM, August 8, 2000, part did. If only we can bring ourselves to look at things this way then we will cease to age, at least psychologically, just as Dorian does physically. And thus far from looming ever larger on the horizon with each tick of the clock, death will become utterly irrelevant as long as we live: just as Epicurus's first consolation claims it is.

But now consider one added feature of Velleman's view of the self. It's a feature that Velleman finds attractive. But in fact it carries a hidden danger.

Say that the 4–5 PM, June 23, 2014, part of your self experiences pain. Even so, Velleman says, it needn't suffer. Suffering comes only from a sense that there is a self that moves ever onward in time, so that the pain it sustains this hour will be compounded by the pain it sustains the next, and the next, and so on. Suppose, however, that you believe that this particular hour's pain is experienced only by that part of your self that occupies this particular hour, and that the next hour's pain is none of its business but is, rather, a burden for the next hour's part of your self to deal with. Suppose you truly live only in the moment—or hour. Then all that you will ever feel at any given moment will be that moment's pain, not any broader suffering.[11]

This sounds good, I guess. But there's a problem. Suppose I adopt Velleman's recommended psychology. Suppose I do begin to treat each hour of my life as occupied by its own distinct part of my self. I leave the previous hour's pain behind and have no concern with the next hour's. Not only do I not age, I don't suffer either. But as Velleman himself acknowledges, most of humankind do not—and probably cannot—look at themselves this way. Most other people, including those closest to me, will continue to see themselves as moving ahead in time, accumulating the previous hour's pain and dreading the next: suffering. Even if I somehow manage to follow Velleman's advice and see myself in the psychologically nonsuffering way he recommends, they won't. And so if I really, truly do come to view my self in the way Velleman proposes, will I not simply write myself out of the common experience of humanity, which in major part is to suffer? Will others not become strangers to me, and me to them? Dead to them, in a way, because numbed to suffering? Even Dorian "suffers" greatly, we are told, because at least he continues to move ahead in time psychologically, if not physically.[12]

By stopping in time while others forge ahead, both Dorian's self (who ceases to age physically if not psychologically) and Velleman's self (who ceases to age psychologically if not physically) lose contact with their fellow human beings. They become statues, or paintings. They lose us and we lose them—in ways that begin to mimic the kind of loss of one another that only death itself, which currently is the sole phenomenon that can part us in time, inflicts.

And so it's an unheralded blessing that we must all move through time together, always occupying the same moment, until we die. If we didn't, aspects of death would come to enter life itself.

Yet although I am glad that we have no alternative but to move ahead in time moment by moment with everyone else, wouldn't it be nice if the precious events in our lives didn't have to vanish back in time moment by moment as they happened? Wouldn't it be wonderful if treasured events, whether we missed them or not, stuck around—as if they were objects like trophies or jewels—for us to cherish and savor and relive?

No, because there'd be a high price to pay. As it is, when a precious event disappears forever into the past—say it's an event I missed, like my daughter's recital—I certainly do feel a sting of regret, perhaps permanently. But I don't feel grief. I know that an event has a life span of whatever moments it takes to happen. But when a precious object like a trophy or a jewel disappears into the past—when, after years or decades, it's destroyed or lost and becomes an artifact of yesterday— then I feel grief, not just regret. Grief is the emotion I experience when something valued that persists in time, not an event that imme- diately vanishes back with time, perishes: dies. And so if events were like objects, with the capacity to remain with me over time at the cost of sooner or later dying to me, disintegrating or losing their sheen just as objects almost always do—then life's losses would, for me, come to resemble death's. There'd be far more grief in my life.

I might feel wistful that the summer in Europe I spent with H in 1983, the moment or experience, is long gone. But it's nothing com- pared to how I would feel if the churches and museums we visited— objects that have lasted centuries—to say nothing of H, who has lasted decades, were suddenly also extinguished. Tom Townsend, the main character in Whit Stillman's movie *Metropolitan*, suffers pangs about all the precious moments his parents missed to be with him when he was a child. But what really gets him is when he sees that they have thrown out his toys—when he sees that precious objects that have somehow managed to survive ever since his youth have finally met their end.

If events persisted in time the way objects do, then their eventual demise would be just as killing. As it is, objects and events relate to each other in a complex emotional ecology. We need them both. Cherished events are with us alas but momentarily, but then while we may feel wistful about their passing, we understand that they are transient and don't usually mourn them.[13] Cherished objects— including other selves—are, thankfully, with us much longer. But when they perish, we feel grief. It's good that we have the mixture.[14]

Joan Didion gives us a sense of what it would be like to treat a precious event as if it were a precious object. She imagines—a bit of magical thinking—that instead of vanishing, like all events do into the past, her own twenty-ninth year actually lived on for decades as a cherished object in her husband's eyes. That was lovely. Until, four decades later, it suddenly died with him. And so, instead of wistfulness over a youthful time long gone in the past, Didion finds herself, as she says, "grieving" and "mourn[ing]" what seems to her to be the death of her forty-year-old twenty-ninth year. After all, it had become a companion in her life—a companion every bit as longlasting as her husband.[15]

Leon Kass, a humane contemporary writer on questions of mortality, makes a virtue of the idea of transience. Perhaps, Kass says, "the beauty of flowers depend[s] on the fact that they will soon wither [like] the fading, late afternoon winter light or the spreading sunset. . . . Does not love swell before the beautiful precisely on recognizing that it (and we) will not always be?"[16]

Kass's poignant observation makes sense when we are talking about events, moments in time. The rose's eclipsed hour of blossoming, the abbreviated instant of the sunset: their briefness before vanishing into the past adds luster to those moments. Such events (if I can be far less poetic than Kass) resemble certain consumer purchases, purchases of experiences, that are more valuable the more fleeting they are. Think of a ticket to a once-in-a-lifetime reunion of the Band.

But objects that persist through time: these we do not want to be transient. Durable purchases like fridges and cars gain value precisely with their endurance and longevity. And when they finally expire they lose their value. If events habitually persisted with us like objects do, whether in actuality or simply in our mind, then their eventual passing, too, would be more destructive than lustrous.

True, one key consolation for mortality, the "Holderlin strategy" discussed in Chapter 2, relies precisely on our learning to treat our life's events—particularly its peak moments of accomplishment, say the high-school basketball championship game twenty years ago—as persisting objects. Let's get our life's pinnacle instances of achievement done as early as possible, the Holderlin strategy advises. That way death, when it comes, will arrive too late to interrupt them. And then let's learn to spend the rest of our time on the planet savoring those moments as we would a trophy or a jewel that stays with us, instead of feeling like a has-been as they slip ever further into the past. That way, we won't experience the itch to embark on new projects that will then be hostage to death. We will thus gain the fullest possible psychological access to Epicurus's second consolation. Once death comes, not only we—but our life—will no longer be here to be harmed by it. After all, it will long since have been happily and sustainingly wrapped up.

Yet this consolation, even if we can manage to find our way to it, comes at a price. It means that we will see life's losses as far more devastating if, for whatever reason, those events that we have treated like objects eventually lose their meaning: if that championship season, with us for so many decades, finally relinquishes its ability to sustain us. For Coach in Jason Miller's play, the big game twenty years before didn't start receding into the past as soon it ended. It remained with him like the trophy itself, enshrined in his living-room cabinet. But then in the course of one catastrophic evening with his now tarnished boys, that "object," that championship season, abruptly shatters. It dies. Coach realizes it's all "history." It was, he says, now speaking in the past tense, "a rare and beautiful thing."[17] And he bewails as anyone would the death of a rare and beautiful thing.

Precisely because for most of us, events—our sweet children's recitals, our championship seasons—vanish immediately into the past, life's losses do not resemble death's. They remain cause more for wistfulness than for grief. And that's a good thing.

I am glad, then, that I am moving ever forward in time, moment by moment, along with all other selves, even toward death. I am glad, in other words, that we are not free to move or stay put as we choose in time the way we can in space. For if we could stop in time as we liked while others moved on, then we would lose each other in life in a way we now can only when we die.

And I am glad that the events of my life, even the most radiant ones, vanish moment by moment into the past, gone as soon as they're done. Yes, knowing that they are ephemeral I often feel wistful as I see them slip back ever further in time. But it would be worse if they somehow stuck around for me to revisit and relive, if they persisted in time the way objects do. Then I would feel real grief when they finally died to me, the way I now do only with objects—and people—when they die.

These two features of mortal existence—that our selves move together relentlessly into the future while the events of our life ceaselessly disappear into the past—are finally what bar life's losses from ever resembling death's. And while that fact doesn't console me about death, it does console me about life.

Four consolatory streams flow at us from the wisdom of the ages. Four strategies offer themselves for our consideration as we seek to reconcile ourselves with our mortal condition. If we look at things in the right way, we will see that:

> Death is benign.
> Mortality gives us all the goods that immortality would.
> Immortality would be malignant.
> Life gives us all the bads that death does.

I have tried to follow each stream on its own winding course and along its various tributaries, commenting on the exotic sights seen along the way. It's when they are taken together, though, that something more deeply revealing emerges. Something that remains invisible from the perspective of each, taken individually, materializes when they are viewed as a whole.

*

We are all moving, moment by moment in time, toward our deaths. And, moment by moment, the events of our lives vanish further and further back into the past. That's how most of us see things. That's our reality. It's what cries out for consolation.

But let's consider the alternatives. And let's not restrict ourselves to realistic options. After all, the question is whether reality itself should leave us disconsolate. Bundles of ego and anxiety that we are, we won't be satisfied if our condition is merely the best that's realistically possible. It has to be the best that's (even barely) conceivable.

So suppose, first off, that we were immortal. But beyond that, nothing else changed. In particular, suppose that we continued, as immortal selves, to move ever forward into the future, while the moments of our lives continued to slip remorselessly behind us into the past.

Would immortality not then ultimately pose its very own choice of deaths?

Consider the possibilities. Suppose, for instance, that our selves, forging ever onward in time, and the events of our lives, flowing ever backward in time, one day ceased to change, to bring us novelty. Suppose that our memories, desires, beliefs, emotional attachments, and commitments—the constituents of our self—no longer evolved. And suppose that the events of our lives, too, all came to resemble the same dull hum. Sooner or later, we'd feel as if we had seen and done all we cared to. Immortality would then take us to a liminal, deathlike realm of stupefying boredom.

On the other hand, suppose that all the memories, feelings, attachments, beliefs, and plans that make up our self, along with all the life events that happened to us, did continuously and thoroughly change and churn and morph and turn over, presenting us with endless novelty. We wouldn't be bored. But then immortality would simply entail a different kind of death: a repeated and utter cutting off of our previous selves and lives, indeed their termination and consignment to oblivion, in favor of new ones.

What if we split the difference? Suppose that we managed to maintain the same trove of memories, values, tastes, feelings, and desires over endless time—so that instead of recurrently dying we remained the same essential self—but that the events of our lives did somehow manage to throw incessant novelty at us, such that we cheated boredom. There'd still be a problem. Immortality would then make us feel ever-increasingly antiquated. We ourselves would have ceased to change while the world and its events continued to, growing ever stranger. There would arise within us an ever-increasingly mournful nostalgia for the past.

By contrast, what if it was our selves that continued to change, regularly jettisoning all previous memories, plans, emotional attachments, beliefs, and desires, while the events of our lives no longer varied but simply came to resemble the same moment repeated over and over? Then immortality would seem to threaten a kind of perpetual dementia.

Immortality, as long as our selves moved ever forward into the future while the events of our lives flowed back ever further into the past, would seem to be a box with no escape—a box whose four walls would comprise grossly distended facsimiles of what we mortals already experience in death and dying. The stuporous sleep of boredom. The complete annihilation of repeated self-disappearance. The ever-deepening antiquated feeling that leads to cascading nostalgia, which one writer likens to a "kind of living death."[1] The futile dementia that spells endless twilight. Immortality, on the twin assumptions that our selves continued moving forward into the future and the events of our lives continued fading back into the past, does look malignant. That's why, when you scrutinize it, you will see that any benign scenario for immortality that fantasists have offered relies on denying one or the other of these two presumptions.

So let's now suppose not only that we were immortal. Let's suppose as well that we no longer had to perpetually move forward in time, while the events of our lives no longer had to recede ever further into the past. What would that look like?

Begin by imagining that we no longer had to move relentlessly forward into the future, moment by moment in lockstep with every other living creature. Imagine instead that we each could disperse as freely over time as we can over space. Suppose, for example, that as an immortal you could stay put for as long as you pleased at your favorite age or year. Meanwhile I, with my own unique needs or preferences, could continue on to a different age or year and then plant myself there for an indefinite spell.

And now imagine too that the precious events of our lives—the time we scaled Everest, the budding stages of a blissful affair—no longer had to slip remorselessly back into the past. Suppose instead that they could somehow remain with us like cherished objects: jewels or talismans that we could fully experience as often as we liked. And then wouldn't immortality be lovely? Wouldn't it be far better than our current mortal lot?

These are hard scenarios to get our mind around. And yet we have some clues. Dorian Gray, in a sense, shows us what it would mean for a self to stop moving forward in time. Dorian opts to cease aging physically if not psychologically. The result, though, is that he utterly cuts himself out of the common experience of humankind. He becomes lost to all others, who do continue moving forward in time. No longer part of the human race, Dorian becomes dead to them.

And that makes perfect sense. After all, in our current reality, if a self stops moving forward in time while others continue on, it could only be because he has died. If we no longer all had to move together moment by moment through time while we were alive, then we would simply begin to lose each other during life in the way we now can only with death.

T. Coraghessan Boyle's short story "The Relive Box" imagines a society in which a new contraption has enabled people to stay as long as they want in a beloved day, week, or month in their life. The result is that family members and friends disengage from each other, die to each other, becoming lost in their own preferred years.[2] Better, then, that we are all compelled to move together, in tandem moment by moment, ever forward in time.

As for preventing a precious event in our life from slipping back in time once it's happened, think again of Coach from *That Championship Season*. He manages to keep his old moment of glory, a long-ago victorious high-school championship game, alive with him as he moves through the decades. He treats it as a cherished object—a psychological if not a physical one like the trophy itself—that he spends time with daily. But then, over the course of one disastrous dinner party with his now debauched middle-aged boys, that precious moment crumbles. It dies to him. And what Coach then experiences is not the mere wistfulness we normally feel as precious moments, which we all know and accept as ephemeral, immediately begin to vanish back in time as soon as they happen. What he experiences is real grief—the kind of grief we feel when we lose a precious object, or person, that has accompanied us for a long time. He goes into mourning.

It is, then, precisely our relentlessly moving together minute by minute into the future, while the events of our lives remorselessly vanish back minute by minute into the past, that saves human life from becoming riddled with intimations of death. If that wasn't the reality, then deathlike losses would begin to permeate life, even if we didn't actually die.

But of course death is our reality. And so various bodies of thought try to console us through a different strategy. They claim that, even within our limited mortal existence, our selves do not necessarily have to move relentlessly forward in time toward our death. Nor do the moments of our lives inevitably have to slip ceaselessly through our fingers into the past. It all depends on how we look at things.

Derek Parfit, for example, advances a Buddhist view. He dismisses, as an illusion, the idea that we are selves moving ever forward, moment by moment, toward death. There is no such self. And hence even though we die, there's nothing that death necessarily destroys. Death, in fact, is benign. It should be far less disturbing to us than it is.

Gordon Bell, the techno-guru, refuses to accept that the events of our lives must necessarily flow ever further back into the past, moment by moment, inexorably out of reach. Instead we can record and digitize every single one of those events—everything we have thought, felt, and experienced minute by minute. We, and especially others on into the unending future, can then repeatedly revisit them. Even though we must die, all the contents of our mind can live on indefinitely, allowing us to gain an intimation of immortality, mortal though we may be.

But consolatory ideas like Parfit's, Bell's, and others I have examined come at too high a psychological price for most of us. I wonder, in fact, whether there's even something deathly about them: whether they give up the game and the ghost at the same time. For us to see death as benign, in the way that Parfit does, for example, we must view our self as already dead. For us to accept that mortality could ever intimate immortality in the way that Bell thinks it can, we must